My Early Life On St. Kitts and Nevis

To PAT

Thanks for visiting

C Sammy Williams

23/Nov/2016

My Early Life On St. Kitts and Nevis

An Autobiography of the First 22 years

CLEMENT BOUNCIN WILLIAMS

authorHOUSE®

AuthorHouse™
1663 Liberty Drive
Bloomington, IN 47403
www.authorhouse.com
Phone: 1-800-839-8640

Published by AuthorHouse   08/24/2012

ISBN: 978-1-4772-6487-4 (sc)
ISBN: 978-1-4772-6485-0 (hc)
ISBN: 978-1-4772-6483-6 (e)

Library of Congress Control Number: 2012915889

Any people depicted in stock imagery provided by Thinkstock are models, and such images are being used for illustrative purposes only.
Certain stock imagery © Thinkstock.

This book is printed on acid-free paper.

DEDICATION

This book is dedicated to the memory of my late
mother and father

Lucille Everette Richards-Williams
&
Benjamin Murray Williams

The inspiration for this book was generated by the number of
questions and concerns posed to me by my son Clement Jomo
Williams A.A.S, B.A, B.S, M.S, O.EE.

THANKS AND ACKNOWLEDGEMENT TO

- My wife Cynthia, my daughter Jihan and my grandson Omoj for their support and encouragement given during the writing of this book.

- My principal editors: Ms. Theresa Nisbett and Mrs. Livian Diamond.

- My early readers: Kenneth Hendrickson, Lorenzo Claxton, Terry Adams, Osbert De Suza, Eustace Arrindell, LeRoy Crosse, Floyd Charles and Unoma Allen who provided the necessary feedback and encouragement.

- All my friends and colleagues who journeyed through those 22 years with me; especially those whose names were not mentioned in the text.

  JFX Studio for the enrichment of the cover designs.

CONTENTS

FOREWORD

St. Kitts and Nevis

St. Kitts and Nevis are two islands within the Caribbean Basin and are part of the eastern archipelago of the Lesser Antilles. They are of volcanic origin with three systems forming the backbone of St. Kitts and a single cone dominating the landscape of Nevis. Their southern shores are washed by the Caribbean Sea and the northern shores by the Atlantic Ocean and they are fanned daily by the tropical breezes of the North Easterly Trade Winds thus maintaining a average year-round temperature of 85⁰ F.

The first inhabitors of these islands were the Carib people and it is believed that they occupied these islands as early as the 2000 years B.C. The first recorded visit by Europeans to these islands was that of Christopher Columbus and his crew on their second voyage to the West Indies in 1492. Thomas Warner, a retired English sea captain, turned Privateer, landed on St. Kitts with a crew of sixteen on a ship called the Hopewell in 1623. Warner landed in the district now called Old Road on the southern Caribbean shores in an area between two rivers that make their exit to the Caribbean Sea within a quarter of a mile. Warner and his group met the Carib people, befriended them and the English were allowed to settle on St. Kitts. Shortly after settling, Warner started to clear lands to grow tobacco from seed he had gotten from the Virginias in the American mainland. His first successful crop of tobacco was harvested in 1625 and he took his bounty of fresh tobacco back to England. Warner managed to get an audience with the King of the day, Charles I and he was granted the title for lands on St. Kitts which established the British Crown Colony of St. Christopher as the first of such colonies in the West Indies. Warner was knighted by the king and was appointed as the first Governor of the colony of St. Christopher. St. Christopher is still the official name for St. Kitts and like many of us Kittitians, we are better known by our nickname than our official names. The name St. Kitts was derived from the fact that one of the English nicknames for Christopher is Kit.

A number of Irish and other European people were brought to these islands to work as indentured servants on the tobacco plantations as they developed. Sugar was introduces as an alternative crop to tobacco sometime around the middle of the seventeenth Century. A large number of African people were brought to these islands to work on the labour intensive tasks of cultivating, harvesting and manufacturing sugar and its by-products such as rum and molasses. The African population eventually outnumbered, by many-fold, all other races of people on these islands. To this day over ninety percent of the population on St. Kitts and Nevis are of African ancestry.

The Colony of St. Christopher flourished and was the centre of the English Colonial operations in the Caribbean for many years. The influx of African slave (unpaid) labour made the economic activities of the island very prosperous. The latter half of the seventeenth and the entire eighteenth century saw many European families accruing great wealth which they repatriated to their metropolitan homelands.

Very early in the nineteenth century the Slave Trade that brought Africans to the Americas and the West Indies was prohibited by law. The Europeans continued to grow the African population by various strategies of selectively breeding the female population with the stronger and bigger males hoping for stronger and bigger off-springs. Slavery was eventually abolished in St. Kitts and Nevis on August 01, 1834. The African people continued to exist as a landless people and were forced to eke a means of survival by working on the plantations of the European landlords for meagre wages and by foraging and growing crops from the fringes of the rainforests and harvesting various forms of sea creatures from the Caribbean Sea and the Atlantic Ocean.

By 1867 the islands of St. Kitts, Nevis and Anguilla, were administered as a single colony for the first time. St. Kitts, Nevis and Anguilla continued to exist as a Crown Colony of Britain with the capital seated in Basseterre, St. Kitts. It was not until nineteen hundred and fifty two (1952) that Adult Suffrage was granted to the entire population of St. Kitts and Nevis; where persons, over the age of twenty one years, were granted the right to vote in popular elections to elect representatives to the Legislative and Executive Councils of the Crown Colony. Prior to Adult Suffrage the qualification for voting in political elections was based on property ownership and income. This qualification barred the majority of the people of African descent from being eligible to vote.

On February 27, 1967 the unitary state of St. Kitts, Nevis and Anguilla was eventually granted a constitutional advancement which provided for an elected parliament with a number of nominated Senators and a Cabinet of Ministers that were responsible for the internal affairs of the State with self governing legislative and executive operations of the islands respectively. This constitutional advancement was labelled as an Associated State to Britain (Statehood) with the local government responsible for all internal affairs with Britain retaining responsibility for Foreign and External Affairs. Shortly after the attainment of Statehood, the Anguillan staged an armed rebellion which eventual lead to the severing of ties with Anguilla.

St. Kitts and Nevis continued as a unitary state until the attainment of full independence on September 19, 1983; with a constitution which labels the union of St. Kitts and Nevis as a Federation. St. Kitts and Nevis is a full member of the United Nation with a vote in the General Assembly and has retained membership in the Commonwealth of Nations that is comprised of the United Kingdom, former British owned territories and dependencies and is still headed by Her Majesty Queen Elizabeth II. The Federation of St. Kitts and Nevis is also part of a number of hemispheric, regional and sub-regional groupings namely The Organization of American States (OAS), the

Caribbean Community (CARICOM) and the Organization of Eastern Caribbean States (OECS).

Sugar continued to dominate the economic activities of St. Kitts and Nevis for over three centuries. Its significance continued to diminish in the latter decades of the twentieth century and the cultivation, harvesting and manufacturing of sugar as a principal economic activity came to an end in 2005. Today the economy of the Federation of St. Kitts and Nevis is driven primarily by tourism related activities, light manufacturing of electronic gadgets and devices, as well as the provision of a number of financial services.

The present population of the Federation of St. Kitts and Nevis is about 52,000 people, St. Kitts (40,000) and Nevis (12,000) on a total land mass of 100 square miles St. Kitts (65) and Nevis (35).

Clement D. O. Williams.

CHAPTER 1

My Maiden Journey to Nevis

My earliest recollection of my life is based on a visit of my Uncle Allan and his wife Sarah to St. Kitts and Nevis in 1953. I remember that I was taken with my mother and father, Uncle Allan and his wife to Nevis. We left St. Kitts on the big boat called "Vagabond".

As I walked onto the pier I was horrified by the fact that I was actually walking over water, because then, the pier was made of wooden planks placed crossways with spaces wide enough that I could see the wave movement of the sea beneath me. I stepped every step that I made in such a manner that my feet would never miss one of the planks, with the fear that if I miss-stepped; I would fall through and end up in the sea. My parents both laughed at me and held my hands in a manner to assure me that I would not fall through those small spaces. My parents walked with such confidence, it made me feel safe.

We got to the boat, my father was the first to get on and he spoke to a tall dark man who was one of the crew of the boat. Uncle Allan then lifted me over the plank at the edge of the pier and handed me to the safe hands of my father, and then Uncle Allan helped Aunt Sarah on and then my mother and he then skillfully skipped onto the boat with ultimate ease. Later he boasted that he had not lost the skill he had acquired in his teenage years as a boy often sailing to St. Kitts with coconuts. Other persons came onto the boat and at the same time the crew was also loading on cargo of rice, flour, cornmeal and other food stuff. All was set for the sailing, passengers were already seated and the sail was hoisted by winches that were nothing but block and tackle pulleys. We sailed out of the Basseterre Harbour mid-afternoon in brilliant sunshine. It was a calm day and we sailed off with great ease. Outside the pier I noticed the boat was going towards the Fort Point, towards the West, and not directly to Nevis that was to the south. I remember asking Uncle Allan why we were going to the Fort and not to Nevis. He said to me that the wind was not blowing right so the boat would have to make tack. Not knowing what that meant it did not bother me because I was in the safe company of my parents and my new found uncle and aunt. It was a long, long sail as the sun had started to fall from the sky. It was not until the darkness had fallen that the boat reached to Nevis. Persons who had traveled with us were angry that they had not gotten home to Nevis earlier. The 'Vagabond' must have had one of its slowest crossings that day. We left the pier in Charlestown and walked up the street for a few yards to the upstairs level of the home of another new-found uncle, Uncle Edmund. Uncle Edmund was so happy to greet us, especially Uncle Allan whom he had not seen for a long time. Uncle Edmund called his wife Eulalie who again was very happy to see us and greeted all of us. Aunt Eulalie prepared supper for us; we had a choice of Vienna sausage or corned beef with bread and hot Ovaltine. I had Vienna sausages, fixed with some kind of sauce that was very delicious. To this day I will choose Vienna sausages anytime ahead of corned beef.

The main purpose of Uncle Allan's visit to St. Kitts and Nevis was to introduce his wife Sarah to the extended family. Uncle Allan had left Nevis in the closing years of 1930's and lived with his wife in Trinidad.

I remembered the next day. We got up early and everyone seemed to be up and about. I went outside of the house where we slept. The environment was strange, with wide open fields and animals of all types were everywhere; chickens, sheep, goats and pigs. I remember asking for the latrine, and was shown an outhouse that seemed miles away. Someone had to follow me. It was different, coming from the inner city slums of Newtown where everything was close but in Jessup, the homestead of my paternal ancestry, the latrine was built as far away as possible from the house. We were at the home of Uncle Son (George) in Jessup; I am not sure how we got there. I guess for the first time I compared and contrasted urban and rural life styles. We had breakfast, but what were most interesting to me were the sugar apples and the deep red, many seeded plums (the type one had to roll and soften so as to make it taste sweet). I remember being introduced to two new cousins; one was about two or three years older than I was and the other a baby in a crib. I remembered the older one as a show-self. He wanted to show his competence in climbing and ran up and down from tree to tree a skill that was remote to me at that time. That was Esmond (George Scarborough—Taxi Operator) and the baby was Austin (former Commissioner of Police). I remembered Uncle Son for his dark complexion and welcoming smile. His wife Rita was of a much lighter complexion and was very friendly.

Uncle Allan and my Father were greeted everywhere they went in the village and received gifts of provisions, eggs and coconuts, a warm welcome for two sons that had returned to their village of ancestry.

We did a tour of the island by car, driven by Uncle Edmond. The thing that has stuck in my memory from that tour was a visit to the New River Estate Sugar factory. My father was hailed as a hero because he was working in the modern Sugar Factory in St. Kitts and by that time had reached the rank of Foreman of the Cane Rake division.

I can vividly remember the return journey to St. Kitts. It was a fair day in brilliant sunshine and a good breeze was blowing. We set sail on the open windjammer called "Valiant". The ride on the Valiant was completely different from that on the "Vagabond". I can recall looking at the bow of the boat as it was cutting through the water. Sometime later I remembered noticing the outline of the Basseterre harbour. As we sailed closer I began to see a landscape that I was familiar with. The oil tanks of Pond's Pasture were first to reveal their full details, the Fort Point, then the almond trees on the bay front, the Government Treasury, the Public Market and then the stores. We sailed back in to the treasury pier in good time. I have always wondered if the names of the boats had any significance to the quality of the trips we had.

CHAPTER 2

My Early Years

My early years were spent in Newtown. My birth was a normal one and home delivery. I had been advised that the attending midwife was a jovial lady whom every one called Nurse West, and who later on in life got married to become Mrs. Archibald. I was told that I weighed ten pound thirteen ounces at birth and this was confirmed some fifty seven years later by Nurse Aurora Turner, who told me that my birth was the first she attended as a student nurse; she vividly remembered the bouncing baby boy and that she had had the pleasure of doing the weighing. I was baptised at the Wesley Methodist Church in Basseterre and was named Clement David Obadiah and was always called by father's surname, Williams.

Life in Newtown was relatively easy for us, when compared with the other people in our environs. My mother was called by her first name, Lucille by her counterparts but all who were younger called her Miss Lucille. My mother was an iconic figure within the community of Newtown. Her principal occupation was that of a huckster and food vendor. She sold many items of provisions, charcoal, salt and homemade confectionaries such as sugar cake, peppermint sweets and ice-cream. She cooked 'tons' of food daily on an open fire fuelled by wood.

The cooking was done primarily in make shift cauldrons made from five gallon tin pans in which kerosene and other products were imported. The main fire place was under a shed that was away from the two-roomed wooden house in which we lived. The fire place was composed of two solid concrete blocks, dimensions of sixteen by twelve by twelve inches on top of which sat two steel rails—made from old locomotive engine tracks, each about five feet long. The wood would be stacked in a particular manner so that when they were ignited they burned along the length of the wood. Secondary fires would use charcoal in coal pots. Wood was acquired from suppliers who cut button mangrove from the swamps of Conaree and Frigate Bay or 'cossha' (acacia) wood from the acacia plants that grew on the pasture land areas. Cossha wood was the premium fuel. Wood was parcelled in bundles and sold in units. In the early 1950's a twenty pound bundle was sold for six pence; the equivalent to twelve cents in Eastern Caribbean Currency.

The main supplier of wood for my mother's industry was an elderly man whose name was Joel Pitt. Mr. Pitt rode a donkey saddled with a dual crook. It was a classic sight to see Mr. Pitt perched on his donkey with two bundles of wood held in the crook on each side of the animal. He made sure that my mother had adequate supplies of her vital fuels, wood and charcoal. The wood which Mr. Pitt brought was always green and freshly cut and filled with moisture. The green wood was left in the sun for several days to dry out. To cook with green wood meant that the fire would be slow and would produce high density clouds of smoke because of the moisture present and a low rate of thermal energy would be given off; contrary to what was required.

A daily routine for my mother would involve cooking a kerosene pan of rice with some form of vegetative mix such as peas, beans, greens, diced breadfruit or pumpkins. Then there was a pan with stewed meat-pork, beef or mutton. Fish was fried on an open dish that was made of a concave piece of cast iron about three quarts of an inch thick and about three feet in diameter. It always appeared black. The black colouring was due to deposits of carbon graphite from the oxidized vegetable oils used in the frying. The graphite layers built-up over a period of time to form a non-corrosive cover on the frying surface. This protected the cast-iron from rusting. This lining or seasoning of the dish is an ancient process that was the precursor of the modern day process of lining frying pans with Teflon.

The local drinks that were made and sold by my mother were principally mauby and ginger beer. The ginger was grated fresh every morning and blended with water to an acceptable strength and then strained (filtered) through the materials of flour bags—a coarse cotton fabric. Complimentary flavouring was added by the use of almond, vanilla and rose essences and it was sweetened to taste with sugar. The mauby had to be prepared the night before. This involved the boiling of a mixture of mauby bark, orange peel, ciliment bush (bay leaf), anise and kockanda root in water to produce a dark concentrated brew. This brew was diluted with fresh water to produce a palatable drink and then sweetened with sugar to taste. It was also important to add quantities of stale mauby that provided the start-up yeast for the fermentation process of the new batch. The fermentation took place overnight and by early morning froth would be foaming over the top of the bottles in which the mauby was placed.

The drinks were dispensed in dark twelve ounce bottles that were previously filled with imported beers, stouts and porters. Popular labels in those days were Tenants, Amstel and Murrays. The daunting task of washing over one hundred half bottles, as they were commonly called, and maybe ten large 750 ml rum bottles was mine. The washing process involved three stages. The first was to shake the bottles with a mixture of a soap solution and bay sand for about ten to fifteen seconds, secondly scrubbing for several strokes with a bottle brush and then the final rinsing with fresh water two to three times.

My mother's major market for her food vending was the Basseterre Sugar Factory. The critical hour was eleven o'clock in the morning, the time when the factory workers got their lunch break. All had to be ready by then, as hundreds of workers had only one hour for lunch. The food and drinks were transported in a box cart with steel bearings used as the wheels. In the early years of my life, this cart was drawn by my older brother Calvin. On the way from Newtown to the breakfast shed at the sugar factory the first stop was at the sugar factory's ice plant to collect ice for the cooling of drinks.

The food was served in enamel bowls and plates, the drinks in makeshift can-cups that were made by soldering a handle onto a juice can. The favourite cans were Trinidad Citrus Growers cans that previously contained grapefruit and orange juices. I guess my mother served about one hundred lunches daily. My mother employed a number of persons to help her, but she was the field marshal doing and supervising everything. The principal help was a young woman whom my mother adopted, her name was Gracie. Gracie lived with us and we all grew up like brothers and sisters.

At the end of the factory session my mother took to the streets of Newtown huckstering for additional sales especially on the Newtown Bay Front where people congregated to purchase fish from the various fishermen and fish vendors. My mother would also use the opportunity at the Bay Front to purchase fish for her trade for the next day. The Bay Front was always abuzz with people in the afternoons. This was the liming spot, where men and women hung-out after a day's work. There was a particular area to the extreme east of the Bay Front that was called 'Lazy Bay'. This was an exclusive male zone where a fair amount of rum drinking and gambling took place.

By early evening my mother would be back at home to finish up the cooked meal that we had for supper. I guess many a day this would be food that was not sold at the sugar factory or the Bay Front. Then it was the routine of work all over again; washing bottles, cutting wood to the appropriate lengths for the fire place, peeling small sweet potatoes and so on.

One of the pastries for dessert was sweet potato pudding. This was made by peeling small potatoes then grating them to a pulp which was then mixed with flour and a sprinkling of raisins and currants. Along with sweet potato pudding, bread pudding was also a favourite. Bread pudding was made by soaking stale bread in water, the soaked bread was then squeezed to remove most of the water; then the pulp was mixed with a sugar, milk and egg mixture and margarine and the usual sprinkling of raisins and currants. Coconut cakes were also part of the menu. The blending or creaming of sugar and margarine was done manually in a large bowl or pot with a wooden pot stick; flour, milk, eggs, grated coconut and baking powder were blended into the mixture. All goods for baking were placed in drip pans and baked in a homemade oven.

The oven was made from a fifty-five gallon oil drum. A door was cut from the curved side of the drum. The door would have a width about three-eighths of the circumference and length about three-quarters of the height of the drum. Hinges were attached to this door and fixed back to the main body of the drum by rivets as well as a latching device was added so as to secure the door. Holes were punched in the body of the drum so as to make layers of shelving by placing three-eighths of an inch steel rod through the holes. The heat for the oven was provided from a coal pot with lighted charcoal that was placed at the bottom within the drum and an additional wood fire would be placed on the top of the drum. All these baked pastries were glazed with a prepared syrup made from water, sugar and spices.

The Friday and weekend specials were ice cream and black (blood) pudding. The mixture for the ice-cream was prepared from custard powder. The required amount of custard was mixed with about one cup of cool water to form a suspension. The bulk of the water was heated in a pot on a charcoal fire on a coal pot; when this water reached to a boil the suspension of custard was added slowly with constant stirring so that the custard mix would not scorch or burn. When the custard was cooked to the required consistency it was removed from the fire and left to cool. The other ingredients of milk, eggs, sugar essences and colouring were added to form the final mix. The cooled mixture was placed in the metal can of the ice-cream freezer (churner) which had a fan like device in the middle. The cover was then placed on the can and the churning mechanism was locked in place. Ice and salt was placed in the outer tub. The churning was done manually. As the churning took place the ice melted and dissolved the salt to form a mild brine which had depressed freezing point and would be about four degrees below zero on the Celsius scale. This caused the custard mixture to attain freezing point and with constant churning allowed only very small crystals to develop; that was responsible for the smoothness of the ice-cream. As the mixture froze it became more and more difficult to turn the handle of the freezer.

Black pudding was made from animal blood, rice and seasoning of scallions (herbs), thyme and pepper. The rice was partially cooked in water and salt. Then the mixture of the ingredients with the partially cooked rice was blended to the required consistency. The mixture was meticulously stuffed into cleaned intestinal tripe of pigs or cattle. The intestines after being thoroughly cleaned, was cut into lengths of about twenty to thirty inches long. One end was first tied with cotton twine or banana flagging, when stuffed; the other end was tied and then placed in boiling water on a fire to complete the cooking. There was a test to tell when the black pudding was cooked. The link was pricked with a pointer from a coconut palm; when no blood was seen oozing out, it was cooked. It was also critical to get the right amount of stuffing, for if the link was over stuffed the boiling process would cause the link to contract and would create a pressure within the link that would cause it to burst; if not sufficiently stuffed the link would become saggy.

I was seven years old when my mother retired from the sugar factory tasks. It was after the birth of her last child, Yvette. My older sister Gwen had taken on the sugar factory side of the business. My mother continued to prepare lunches and dinners for a selected number of persons which she dispensed from her home. She continued to sell her confectioneries and pastries from her home and at the Newtown bay front. She also continued her Friday and weekend specials of ice cream and black pudding. My mother was well to do compared to other families in our environs.

Up to this point my oldest sister Gwen had still lived at home with my mother even though she had a number of children. Gwen worked with my mother and never had to seek employment outside the home. After a while however, there was some discord between Gwen and my mother, and Gwen was summarily discharged from our home. She and her children moved to Pond Site to live with my grandmother. By the time my mother retired her services from the sugar factory, Gwen was in a position to take on that task. She set up her business and continued in a line of succession of family women who sold food at the sugar factory. There was my grandmother Marion Thomas and then my mother Lucille Richards followed by my sister Gwendolyn Green. The sense of an independent living, supported by the gift of enterprise had transcended through four or five generations. For today, the baton is carried by Gwen's daughter Marlene who sells the same commodities from the back of her Toyota Crown Saloon car, a far cry from the box carts of the previous generations.

My second sister Rita had also been at home with the family. She died from the complications of pregnancy. I remembered the wake that was held the night before the burial. A number of well wishers came to the home to give condolences and stayed on for the ceremony of the wake. They drank rum and coffee and ate crackers till the wee hours of the fore-morn singing hymns appropriate for the occasion.

The day of the funeral, her body was removed from an ice chest. This was a wooden box that had an inner container made from galvanized zinc, in which the corpse was placed and then an upper chamber in which ice was placed so as to keep the corpse at an ambient temperature to reduce the rate of decomposition. There were no electric freezers available for storing the dead. Generally, burials were done by the day after death. A practice which was used by persons, who could not afford to pay for the ice chest, was to cover the corpse with sea-weed and occasionally sprinkling the corpse with sea-water. The salinity of the sea water and the constant moistening was sufficiently effective in preserving the dead for a day.

The coffin was made by a carpenter who lived on Roxborough Street. My mother journeyed with the carpenter early in the morning to Horsford's Lumber Yard to select the board for making the coffin which she paid for. I was with my mother then. By afternoon everything was ready. Godmother, Iris Crossman another woman of iconic character, a seamstress by profession made the shroud in which they dressed the corpse of my sister Rita, to make her ready for burial. I can remember the gathering standing outside our house at Roxborough Street posing for a photo with the departed. The burial was at the Springfield Cemetery.

My only brother on mother's side was Calvin. He was the work horse. He tended a flock of sheep. His routine was to take the sheep to Pond's Pasture to graze; where he would hammer metal or wooden stakes in the ground and tied the adult ewes in a position where they could get sufficient food for the day. The rams and the lambs were free to roam. By evening time, just before the sun set, he would go to collect his sheep. An incident that caused my first appearance at the Magistrate Courts took place on a Saturday morning when I had the privilege to go with my brother to tie out the sheep. That morning a man named Norris Techeira, a baker, came out of his bakery and started to beat my brother with the flat side of a machete in a way not to cut him but to inflict some heavy blows (planance) on my brother. The matter was reported to the police and the matter went to court. Mr. Techeira's defence was that the day before my brother had struck his dog with the four pound hammer which my brother used to hammer the stakes to tie his sheep. My brother's counter to that point was that the dog was attacking his sheep and he threw the hammer to ward off the dog. The hammer did hit the dog. My first appearance in court came when I was called as a witness for the plaintiff. The lawyer representing my brother was the late Franklyn Adams. Mr. Techeira was convicted and had to pay costs to the courts and compensation to my brother for injuries sustained. At that time the Magistrate's Court was on the second floor of the Newstead Building on the south-western corner of Church and Central Streets.

In those days most people in Newtown went to the public stand pipes to get supplies of water. My brother would use his box cart with several pans and buckets to get water. After each trip he would take the pans and buckets into the yard and dump the water into an oaken barrel. It was a delight when we had overnight rains, because a spouting from the house channelled the water from the rainfall into the barrel. His other task was to pound stone to various sizes for the aggregates of the masonry industry; especially for the road works that were still going on as part of the Slum Clearance. He got rocks from the foothill of the Eastern Range, just above the area now known as Bird Rock, as well as from the seashore. The large rocks were shattered to smaller and more manageable pieces by hitting them with a ten pound sledge. The smaller pieces were further degraded to fine stone—about one inch bits and coarse stone—about inch and a half to two inches. The Public Works' truck would come to buy the various aggregates by the barrels. This was the main source of his income.

Shortly after leaving school his eyesight started to fade; he continued his industry in spite of fading sight until he died at the age of twenty one. His problem was diagnosed to be a brain tumour that was pressed on the optic nerves. The growth of the tumour eventually caused his death. Another funeral experience for me and it was a carbon copy of the events that took place for my sister Rita's funeral.

Aunt Catherine was the person who took care of the laundry of the household. She was not a blood relative but a good friend of my mother. She had no children of her own and treated us all the younger ones as her own. She lived across town and came every morning to help with the preparations of the food. By the time the hustle and bustle of the eleven o'clock hour was over her task was to stay, clean up and start the washing and other aspects of the laundry works. In those early years Aunt Catherine washed everything manually in an oaken tub or galvanized bath-pan. She used a scrubbing brush on tough material and rubbed manually on a washing board that had groves cut transversally across the body of the board. Bar soap, of high caustic content was used. Bar soap came in the colours of brown or blue and was sold in the shops by the penny-lengths. A milder soap was used for more delicate pieces and fabrics such as nylon and silk. The popular brand of the milder soap was "Sunlight". Aunt Catharine pressed the laundry with flat irons that were heated on charcoal fire in a coal-pot. When the irons were hot enough, they were wiped with a rag so as to remove any trace of soot or debris that the face of the irons might have picked up during the heating process. Sometimes she used a goose. This was a devise with a hollow cavity in which charcoal was packed and lit. The goose had a flue hole which allowed air to get to the burning charcoal and a neck with a wide mouth which acted as an exhaust that allowed the products of combustion between the air and the charcoal to escape. The bottom of the goose was flat and was the place where the heat was concentrated.

It was imperative that all garments of importance as well as tablecloths and sheets that were made from cotton and linen be starched before ironing. The starch used was made from locally grown cassava; the powdered starch was cooked into a gel by pouring a suspension of the starch in cold water, into hot boiling water. The laundry piece was then soaked in the gelatinous mixture and then hung out on the clothes line to dry. Before a starched piece of garment was ironed, it was moistened by sprinkling the fabric with water and then it was rolled into a ball so as to have the moisture evenly distributed though the piece of garment. Ironing then was a most tedious task, but after the introduction of electricity into Newtown, we got an electric iron (heater) that made Aunty Catherine's task much lighter.

Every yard had a stone bleach which was used to help remove stains and mildew from garments, sheets and tablecloths. The item to be bleached was laid out flat on the stone bleach on a sunny day at the height of the sun; these items were drenched with clean water that initiated a photochemical reaction between the water, the oxygen from the atmosphere and the sunlight to render the colouration of the stains or mildew to a colourless substance. Stains such as 'iron mole' were caused by deposits of ferrous rust; they were bleached by placing salt and lime juice on the area of the stains. The salt and lime juice reacted chemically to produce hypochlorous acid which decomposed to release active oxygen atoms that did the bleaching.

My father was a visiting dad. He lived in his own property at Shaw Avenue, Mc Knight. He worked as a foreman at the Basseterre Sugar Factory and was in charge of the number 2 shift at the cane rake—later to become the cane dump with the advent of hydraulic modernization. In the off or dull season he was the head painter and managed all the painting jobs for the entire sugar factory on site as well as offsite. This involved the painting of railway bridges and water tanks all over the Island.

I can remember that one Friday night my father took me on his bicycle from Newtown to Mc Knight so that I could sleep with him because he wanted to take me to a water-tank at Golden Rock Estate just north of the airport the next day. The Sugar Factory had just constructed a huge water tank there to store water for their operations at the factory. The Saturday morning my father and I got up early and had breakfast. We started our journey to his work site, for that day at Golden Rock. His bicycle, a Hercules male frame with 28 inch wheels was our transport. I sat on the cross bar and he pedalled our way to Golden Rock. The group of men whom my father was supervising were painting the outside surface of the water tank with silver paint. I carefully climbed the riggings until I eventually reached the top. It was a fantastic sight to see Basseterre and the extended areas of the Basseterre Valley; from the horizon on the Caribbean Sea to the south the Eastern and Northern Ranges of mountains and the volcanic system of Mount Oliveese locking in the Basseterre Valley. The verdant fields of sugar cane, the dense green slopes of the mountains covered with tropical rainforest, provided postcard views in every direction.

I always wanted to go to Golden Rock Estate area. The boys from the St. Peters area who went to the Basseterre Boys told several tales about wild rabbits and guinea pigs that made the area there their habitat. I was anxious to see some of these wild creatures. After coming from the top of the water tank I started to search the area within the vicinity of the tank. To my greatest disappointment the only wild animals that I saw were a number of mongooses that came around expressly to get the scraps from the workers lunch. It was an interesting day at Golden Rock, particularly in seeing the type of work my father did outside of the Sugar Factory.

He came to Newtown every evening for his supper.

He came to St. Kitts from Nevis at the tender age of fourteen. Jessup's Village was his ancestral home. He first settled at Milliken Estate within the St. Peter's Parish. As he progressed, he moved from the fields and cattle sheds of Milliken Estate to the Basseterre Sugar Factory. My father worked at the sugar factory for over forty five years. When he eventually retired, he received a weekly pension of nine dollars and ten cents in nineteen sixty five.

My father was one of the early pioneers in the Labour Movement. By the time of the famous thirteen weeks strike (1948) of the Basseterre

Sugar Factory he was the secretary of the Sugar Factory section of the St. Kitts Nevis Trades and Labour Union. My understanding is that he was the man on the spot that called the stoppage of work and led the workers out of the sugar factory. This period of thirteen weeks must have been very trying for my parents as my father was in the thick of things pertaining to the strike and my mother was pregnant with me.

By the resolution of the strike, my father was one of the few instigators who got back their job at the Sugar Factory.

CHAPTER 3

Slum Clearance and Electrification

It was sometime in the early fifties, shortly after Adult Suffrage was attained in 1952, that an effort was made to transform the social and health conditions in St. Kitts. The first elections of 1952 saw five representatives-who were elected by the people of St. Kitts, joining the administrator in council to form the Executive of the Crown Colony Government of the day. The five representatives were assigned portfolios. Amongst them was Maurice Davis, a lawyer later to become the Chief Justice of the Supreme Courts of the Organisation of Eastern Caribbean States and eventually knighted by Her Majesty Queen Elizabeth. The Honourable Maurice Davis then had the responsibility for Communications and Works.

The slum clearance program for the inner city was a priority. The slums of Newtown were reorganized and the alley ways were widened to make paved streets of asphalt and concrete with the appropriate drainage. Many of the houses were removed to develop the project of Pond Site. The Pond Site Housing project was developed by the Central Housing Authority (CHA) for the purpose of providing land and houses for the persons that were displaced from Newtown. Previously the land area of Pond Site was a sugar cane field. The layout of Pond Site was done by the engineering staff of the Public Works Department. The streets were named after the early stalwarts of the Workers League—later to be renamed the St. Kitts Nevis Labour Party. At Pond Site the streets are Manchester Avenue, Sebastian Street, John Street, James Street and Neverson Street along with East Street and West Street.

At the time of the initial slum clearance, our family lived in a two room wooden house. My mother's was one of the houses that remained at Mad House Alley. Our boundaries were pushed inwards and we were compensated with land to the North. My grandmother Marion Thomas had her house removed from the slums to Pond Site. The clearance transformed the slums to a well laid out project with Caunt Street, Shepherd Street, Carty Alley (Semper Street), Roxborough Street and many paved walkways opened up easy access to the houses.

In those days very little solid waste was generated by the domestic household. Most persons cooked foodstuff that were locally produced; ground provisions such as pumpkin, peas, sweet potatoes, yams, cassava, tannia, dashene, eddoes and breadfruit were the main vegetable staples. In addition to these vegetables, cornmeal, rice and flour provided the main carbohydrate sources of our diets. When one went to the shops to purchase these commodities, one had to take separate containers in which they were collected and reusable shopping bags were always used. The luxury of pre-packaged goods and the excessive amount of plastic bags used in modern day shopping were nonexistent. The peelings from the vegetables were reserved for the pigs, sheep and goats that were kept by many persons within the environs. Whatever domestic solid waste was generated was stored in trash pans and placed outside the various homes.

The solid waste collection in Newtown at around the time of the slum clearance was done by an elderly gentleman named Mr. Alfred with a cart drawn by his single horse Ned. The trash was collected and dumped at the top end of Ponds Pasture where there were several swamps. This area was the official dumpsite for the Basseterre area. It was not until after the paved roads were established that the Public Health Department dump trucks came through the Newtown area to collect solid waste.

Ned was the most docile horse that one could find. He allowed the boys of Newtown to pull the hairs from his tail without a fuss. We even described Ned as the wooden horse. The boys used the horse hairs to make traps for the pond birds (sandpipers) that frequented the ponds on Ponds Pasture.

The sandpipers were also shot with catapults. The boys would pluck the feathers from their catch and remove the guts and roasted them in open fires or fried them in makeshift frying pans. The cooked birds provided a treat for many of the youngsters in Newtown.

Many families were encouraged to do some expansion on their properties. My mother did a major addition to our house. She had constructed to the north a wooden structure measuring twelve by eighteen feet which was divided in two rooms one eight by twelve that served as a bedroom and the larger ten by twelve feet served as the living room. To the west and adjacent to the living room was an addition for a verandah and a single one bedroom unit that was detached from the rest of the house with separate entrance. This room became rented quarters. The first tenant to occupy this room was a man who every one called 'Mos-so'. He worked at the sugar factory and was originally from the village of Saddlers.

It was convenient for him to get a rented room in town as public transportation back to Saddlers at ten in the evening was nonexistent. It also gave him the opportunity to enjoy some of the bliss of urban life. He drank a lot of hard liquor. He would visit his relative in the country from time to time on some weekends. Unfortunately for him one weekend he might have overdone the drinking and passed away in his sleep. Unnoticed for several days, it was not until the Monday afternoon after my curiosity caused me to investigate the buzzing of blue flies; and I peeped through the window, that I discovered the lifeless body of the big man with a pale complexion. He had become one of my favourite people. He always had the goodies of fruits and sugar cane for me on his return from his usual visits to his home village. Incidentally this was the first of two lifeless males, living alone, that I had come to discover.

Sometime in the early nineteen fifties the program of electrification started and for the first time street lamps were erected in the Newtown area. A number of homes were wired to accommodate the expansion of electrification. A new power plant was erected at Needsmust estate and it was producing alternating current (ac) unlike the old generators that were located in the middle Central Street, Basseterre that produced direct current (dc). There were two buildings owned by the government on the Central Street site. The one to the east housed the power generating sets and the other to the west was the ice plant and cold storage facility. The electricity produced by this plant was dc current. The electricity that was produced then was distributed only to the upper echelons of society like the planters and merchant classes for their homes and businesses. There were a limited number of street lamps in the inner city of Basseterre. Our home was one of two to get electricity on Roxborough Street when the lines were electrified. The other was the home of our neighbour immediately to the north. That house was occupied by a couple who were Mr. and Mrs. Roland Hull. Mrs. Hull was a mulatto of high yellow complexion and we all referred to her as the white lady. She was a seamstress of note. Shortly after electrification she had her sewing machine adapted to operate with an electric motor. Mr. Hull was a machinist at the Sugar Factory and he rode his bicycle to and from the sugar factory. The bicycle was his means of transport.

We were the first to have a huge cabinet radio with gramophone and built in speakers. The model was 'Sobell' and it was bought from the distributor Mr. Norris Caines whose businesses operated on Fort Street. My father brought a number of records, the large discs that spun at seventy eight revs per minute (78r.p.m.); the favourite tunes were from Lord Kitchener and the Roaring Lion from Trinidad and Ivan Brown from Montserrat. People came to stand outside our house to listen to these records. On a number of special occasions my mother put on what was called a house dance. Persons paid a fee to get in. The dancing area was the addition to the North of the property where all chairs, beds and tables were removed to provide adequate space for the public event. The entrance fee was one shilling (24 cent EC). The verandah was used as the space for hanging out (liming). Hard liquor, beer and food were sold in a make shift tent out in the back yard. It was simple but people enjoyed themselves. It was common to have over one hundred persons mingling at these house dances; those who could not afford to pay the entrance fee stood on the adjacent side-walk to listen to the music and were also permitted to go to the tent in the backyard to purchase drinks and food. All advertisement for these dances was done by word of mouth-" Lucille gon' have a dance next Saturday night". Persons also came to our house to get the scores of the West Indies Cricket team doing battle down-under in Australia as well as in England. It was my task in later years to write the end of play scores on a chalk board that hung from our verandah. It was to our home that the arrangers of the famed Invaders Steel Band came to listen to records and copy the tonic sulpha for the various parts for the orchestration of their renditions.

We were the first home on Roxborough Street to have pipe borne water. My mother paid for several lengths of half inch galvanized pipe to bring the water from the water mains at Cayon Street. We had two sinks built from concrete placed adjacent to the kitchen with a single tap over the chamber to the right when facing the tap and an outside bath room with an overhead shower. It was a great relief for us not having to go to the public stand pipe to head and cart tons of water daily. My mother permitted some of the neighbours to come to her yard to fetch water that saved a journey to the nearest public stand pipe at the corner of Branch and Cayon Streets. Persons came to our bath and paid one penny to bathe. At that time most persons who wanted a full bath had either to journey to the public baths at the Newtown Bay Front or near Bakers Corner or did it on a stone bleach, within their yard, with water fetched from the public stand pipes.

Sanitation was deplorable in the slums of Newtown. It was common to find human faeces in the alleyways at morning, because persons used the cover of darkness to ease their bowels in convenient spots. Many persons held it and went to the neighbouring cane fields or the sea shore. Many homes had a bucket, which was lodged under a seat in an outhouse privy. The men and women of the night-soil crew came long after dark to collect the filled buckets and took them to the Newtown seashore to dump the raw sewage in the sea. There are many classical tales about the adventures of the night-soilers. The average cost to dump a bucket was about three pence (6cent EC). There were professional night-soilers who made a living from that. After the slum clearance most households started to dig pit toilets. A hole was dug manually in the earth for over twelve to fifteen feet deep and diameter of about three feet; the top was fitted with a collar and seat made from concrete in specially designed moulds. These concrete structures were purchased from the Basseterre Public Health Centre at the Gardens, Mc Knight. I can remember when our first pit was dug; it went down as far as the water table.

Parasites such as lice, fleas, jiggers and bed-bugs were common place. Bed bugs were of a particular nuisance. They sucked the fluid of life directly from your body; their only means of nutrition was human blood. By the mid fifties DDT, an insecticide, was introduced in St. Kitts. It was common to use a mechanical flit gun with DDT to control the infestations of bed bugs. There were special periods when the Health Inspectors came around with high pressure pumps to fog the houses with DDT and other insecticide fumes to get rid of not only bedbugs but mosquitoes and cockroaches. During the rainy seasons, mosquitoes that bred in the swamps at Ponds Pasture found their way into the Newtown community. These vectors of such diseases of yellow fever, dengue and malaria were omnipresent. There was very limited vaccination and the rate of infant mortality was very high. Many adults also fell victim of these deadly diseases. By the mid fifties large scale public drives were staged to boost the immunization of all persons. The schools were the centre of focus. One local remedy to get rid of mosquitoes was to have a fire that was smothered with green leaves from plants. The high moisture content of the green vegetation gave off high density smoke and it was common to see many smoke pits in the community. One could only guess the devastation from the smoke with respect to persons who suffered from lung diseases such as asthma.

CHAPTER 4

The Letter Writer

My mother said that she went to the Basseterre Girls School for her basic elementary education and left at the end of standard Five. She left school to work with my grandmother Marion Thomas whom every one called Narna. My mother, in her later years in school was given permission from the headmistress of the Girl's School to leave school at break time to be at the Sugar Factory for eleven o'clock daily to help with the distribution of the lunches as well as to wash the dishes. By one o'clock she had to be back in school for the rest of the afternoon session. My mother had an immaculate hand writing; her letters were upright with a cursive style. An elementary education up to fifth standard in those days was of extreme value.

Sunday was the day of rest for my mother. Her routine then would be to clean up from late Saturday night's business and prepare Sunday meal for the family. After lunch she would refresh herself with a shower and would rest for about two hours. She would take her Bible to bed with her; I don't think she would read too much, the labours and burdens of the week demanded that period of rest. By mid-afternoon she started another career, letter writing. In the early fifties a number of persons had migrated to England to better their conditions of life. The principal means of communications in those days was by mail. Letters were delivered daily by a postman who either walked about or rode a bicycle to cover his route. Many of the mothers, fathers and spouses whose loved ones had ventured abroad could not read nor write.

They came and waited their turn in line. It was like an office of any professional with their clients. The table in the bedroom was partially cleared and my mother sat on the long side of the table with her client on the corner to her left. Client and letter-writer relationship was important. My mother would have a writing pad, ink and blotting paper at hand. She used a special fountain pen that one of her adopted wards sent for her from England; I remembered the brand to be "Esterbrook". She read the letters in the privacy of her 'office' and would draft an immediate response. The clients explained what they wanted to communicate in dialect and my mother would translate it to Standard English and wrote the appropriate thoughts. The alternative to writing paper and envelope was an aerogram commonly called a letter form. These were ideal for short letters and cost much less than a half ounce sealed letter and envelope. Those days an aerogram cost six pence (12 cents EC) to mail to anywhere in Europe or America. It was one in, one out in a continuum into the night when the lights had to be turned on. Stamps and letter forms were sold at Mr. Bias' shop on Pond Road and immediately opposite to the northern entrance to Roxborough Street. I never found out what my mother's fees were for letter writing, but I knew that she was compensated in some way; parcels with goodies, like sheets, cutlery and clothing came regularly. Frequent enclosures in registered letters from England were money orders, some for as little as five shillings ($1.20 EC) some as grand as ten pounds sterling ($ 48.00EC). These remittances were vital for the survival of many of the older folks.

My mother was a money lender. She had helped quite a number of persons to go to England by lending them money to help pay their passages to England. Many repaid with good interest but the opposite was also true, many of those who went were never heard from for several years.

My mother was not a regular Church goer. She had a firm Methodist religious upbringing and was a firm believer in Christian principles. Her pace of work just never afforded her the time to be regular at church. She always said her prayers at nights and mornings. She read her Bible now and then but she always had her radio tuned to WIVV, a religious radio station that was based on Vieques, Puerto Rico. She always listened to the early morning Don and Dave Show.

Don and Dave were religious commentators who gave their views on world events from a religious perspective and interspersed their commentary with hymns and requests from listeners.

I never saw my mother read a newspaper, magazine or book other than the Holy Bible. Apart from the few school books I had, there were only two other books in the house. They were The Holy Bible and a Jehovah's Witness book which she had bought from a neighbouring gentleman whose name was "Hammy" Thomas. I never saw my mother read the Jehovah's Witness book; it was thick in excess of five hundred pages with a green, hard cover. I can remember the time when the world was to come to an end; one of the predictions that was given by the time setters. It was to be a Sunday at three o'clock in the afternoon. I can vividly remember, my mother and I had our Sunday bath and went to bed. My mother never seemed to be bothered by the predictions because she slept soundly for her usual Sunday siesta. I sat up in the bed and kept watching the clock on the china cabinet as the long and short hands moved, closer to three o'clock. I guess I heard every tick of the clock; the entire area was still and silent. My anxiety began to grow as the short hand was edging closer towards the number three digit on the white face of the dial and the long hand started the ascent towards twelve at the summit of the dial. I kept looking at my mother who must have been miles away in dreamland. The hour came, nothing happened. The calmness of the atmosphere and the absence of sounds from the environment caused me to believe that something was really going to happen and maybe our clock was a little too fast. I watched the alarm bell at the top of the clock, it was silent, there were no vibrations or tremors that I was certain to come. In fact, I guess I had mixed feelings about the failure of the prediction that was to date and time the end of the world.

My mother awoke from her sleep. I remember telling her that the world did not end. She smiled and assured me that no man will know the date and time when God would come for his world. By four o'clock one could hear the bustle and noise of the inner city slums of Newtown back to its usual din and tenor.

CHAPTER 5

Early Schooling

My early schooling was done at Mrs. White's Private School. Mrs. White was a tall lady of light complexion whose principal career was in nursing. When she retired from the Public Service she continued to practice as a mid-wife and opened her private pre-school. Shortly after my joining of Mrs. White's school she decided to close her school; but I was kept on as the sole student, receiving individualized instructions. By the age of seven I was able to do long divisions, dividing any number by three and four digit numbers. I had learnt multiplication tables up to fifteen times. This was the foundation for my love for mathematics. My mother bought all the 'abc' books and primers and Mrs White and I worked through every page. I was able to read at a very early age. Many a day I sat at a desk in a corner of Mrs. White's kitchen. My assignments were given and I had to work through whatever exercises were assigned as Mrs. White went about her daily chores.

Mrs. White, her three daughters, a son in law and a nephew all lived in the upstairs section of a big house on Mad House Alley. I have been told that the house was used as the Lunatic Asylum for St. Kitts before the institution was moved to Haynes Smith Village on Cardin Avenue; hence the name Mad House Alley. Our home was adjacent to the north of the former Mad House, so my journey to school involved the shortest trek, which was to walk through the fence via a makeshift gate. The other children who had left Mrs. White's School went to Newtown Infant School that was held in the lower section of the Odd-Fellows Lodge at the corner of Pond Road and Sandown Road.

January 1956, I was enrolled at the Basseterre Boys' School. I was taken to the school by my father. At that time I was staying with my father at his house in Shaw Avenue, Mc Knight as my mother was hospitalised at the Cunningham Hospital for a period of time after she had given birth to my sister Yvette. My sister was born on December 17, 1955 and my mother was not released until sometime in the second week of January 1956. I guess that there were some complications at or after the birth of my sister that caused my mother to be detained at the Hospital for a protracted period of about three weeks. The headmaster at Basseterre Boys' was Mr. William F Dore. Since I did not come through the regular infant school system I had to go through a vigorous interview. Mr Dore decided that he would place me in second standard where my class teacher was Miss Inez Walters. Most of the classmates were bigger and older than I was; those were the days when one had to pass the examinations to move up to the next standard. I was seven years then but I am certain that there were boys older than ten in the same class. Even though I was always big for my age I had no choice but to stand in the front row. My closest friends and I turned out to be the three C.W.'s, Cedric Woodley, Calvin Woods and Clement Williams.

We went back to Newtown when my mother was released from the hospital. For the first week or so my mother followed me to the top of Roxborough Street at the junction with Pond Road and instructed me to wait for Eulic Jones or Lassalle "Shine" Maynard to take me to school. These two turned out to be my guardians at Basseterre Boy's for at least the first term.

Miss Walters was an attractive lady who wore spectacles; she had her own strap and used it excessively. Life in Boys' School was completely different to what I knew at Mrs. White's. I was in a class of seventy students and lost the comfort of individualized instructions. I was lost in Dictation and Spelling, but Arithmetic both mental and computation were so easy. I can remember Miss Walters teaching long multiplication; labouring the concepts of alignment of units, tens, hundred and thousand and the addition in line. The class struggled to learn, but I was laughing because I had done that at Mrs. White maybe a full year before. I had my sums—as we called all computation then already worked and correct. I struggled with Dictation and Spelling. I got lashes for every Spelling and Dictation exercise and cannot remember ever getting a single lash for Arithmetic, whether mental or computation. I tutored my friends in arithmetic. Every six weeks or so we had special tests, I was always in the middle ranks of the class.

The giants of our class were Vincent Liburd, Desmond Herbert I, Desmond Herbert II, Desmond Hanley and Raphael Payne; those guys scored consistently in all areas. Despite my perfect marks in Arithmetic, my failing grades in Spelling and Dictation would drag me to the middle of the rankings. At the end of the school year, the Inspectors of School came with standardized tests. Every other boy in the row was assigned to take Spelling and Dictation and the next was given Arithmetic. Fortunately for me Cedric Woodley and I were sitting adjacent to each other. During the assignment of subjects, Spelling and Dictation fell on me. Cedric and I made a switch in the seating arrangement; the outcome of which saved me from becoming a second standard grandfather. We both did well in our respective fields on the standardized tests. We were both in the group that skipped to 4B rather than going to standard three.

Class 4B was taught by an eccentric lady named Miss Wade. She was a Montserratian by origin and was sister to Mr. Lynch Wade Inspector of Police. Miss Wade was a tall dark lady who wore simple clothing and not much makeup except for lipstick. She had an exquisite hand writing. Her lessons in penmanship were remarkable; stressing the importance of straights and curves when forming letters and digits and with some flourish by pressing light on the up strokes and heavy on the down strokes. By the time we were in 4B the Headmaster of the school was Mr. James Sutton. Mr Sutton was also a craftsman in penmanship. He took much interest in the way the boys wrote and instituted a regime of punishment for boys who did not write well. I never got punished for penmanship because I practised under the tutelage of the two best teachers of penmanship. Many years later my wife always commended my handwriting and the lyrical content of our many letters, but many a times and over she had to forgive me for the poor spelling. I made lots of efforts to learn to spell, bought the Sensible Spelling Book, but somehow never got the art right.

After 4B was 4A. We had a Mrs. Warner for class teacher. She was a short dark lady, very much in the structure and build of my mother Lucille. The three CW's were still together. We sat together along the side bench. Mrs Warner's strap was dreaded. One day Mrs. Warner wrote some work on the board for us to do. By then we had understood the principle of division of labour and we always completed our work within time. This day, having completed the assignment we got involved in some extra-curricular activities. Mrs. Warner with her strap and the power of the woman, let go a single swing with her strap that had all three of us jumping and prancing. That was a case of three-at—a blow. Apart from that our year with Mrs. Warner was a routine one.

In fifth standard, it was Mrs. Elzera Edwards who was our class teacher. By then, they had added Elementary Science and Hygiene to the curriculum. This gave me more prowesses and by this time I had started to feature in the top quadrant of the class. The mark sheet was totalled of seven hundred as the curriculum expanded and particularly in the subjects of my liking. Mrs. Edwards was the teacher of my choice in Basseterre Boys'. She was very strong in Arithmetic and Elementary Science and did some of the practical experiments in the Elementary Science Workbook. I loved my year in fifth standard. By then the only separation in marks between the guns and I were the difference in marks in Spelling and Dictation.

My final year at Basseterre Boy's was in standard six, where the teacher was Mr. Errol Bowens. We did every concept in Arithmetic and a very basic introduction to Algebra. Mr Bowens was a real master, he appeared to know everything. His efforts in Singing and Poetry were outstanding. We sang many of the classical nursery rhymes and folksongs. The two that reverberate in my mind are 'My Grandfather's Clock' and 'Golden Slippers'. Sometime in 1960 six standard and seven standard classes were allowed to occupy the first block of the new school that was built east of the Grammar School and was to be named The Basseterre Senior School. The population of the Basseterre Boy and Basseterre Girls were exceeding the capacity of the church buildings that had served for decades as open hall schools. Standard Seven was taught by Mr. Suswin Mills.

In standard six we learnt all about L.C.M., H.C.F., G.C.M. and square roots. We calculated all the arithmetical functions of many numbers, all manually. It was in my final year at the Cave Hill Campus of the University of the West Indies, Barbados in a Number Theory class, when the professor introduced an algorithm; a step by step process that had to be followed exactly to get the correct outcome, that I met a process that I had learnt some twelve years earlier. This algorithm was the process by which one can calculate the square root of any real positive number, whether whole or decimal fraction or mixed with combination of whole and decimal. Everyone in my class at UWI was taken aback to know that I understood the process instantly. It was not that I was a genius but I had done that in standard six under the tutelage of Mr. Bowens. I have not learnt a new arithmetical concept beyond what I knew when I left Basseterre Boys'.

Basseterre Senior School was ready for its first intake, January 1961. All the boys and girls from the Basseterre Valley and St. Peters over the age of twelve were to be admitted. A screening test was given to all students to determine the placement of students in forms. The subjects examined were English, Spelling and Dictation, General Knowledge and Arithmetic. The tests were administered in two batches as fate would have it; I was in the second batch for Spelling and Dictation. One of my best friends Emrod Martin was in the first batch, overnight I was able to brief him on the Arithmetic and he gave me an insight into what words to expect on the spellings. With the aid in spelling it was no surprise to me that I was placed in 1A, the top group for students who were born in 1948.

Our form teacher in 1A was Mrs. Matilda Warner, a tall, powerfully built woman of very light complexion. Unlike at Basseterre Boys where we had one teacher for everything, at Basseterre Senior School, there was the form teacher who was responsible for the administrative matters pertaining to the form and there were other teachers who came in to teach the various subjects. The mathematical subjects, Arithmetic, Geometry and Algebra were taught as separate subjects and each was scored on one hundred percent on the mark sheets, this was to my natural advantage and gave me a more competitive edge. All three mathematical subjects were taught by Mrs. Warner.

After about two weeks at Basseterre Senior, the system of monitors was introduced; each class had two monitors, one male and one female. Form 1A had Greta Prince and I were appointed as the first monitors. The job of the monitor was to do everything teachers did except teaching. We had to keep order, oversee the sweeping of the class and make sure all curricular materials were stacked and locked away in the cabinets at the front of the class. With the responsibility also came the authority, monitors made a list of the culprits and reported them to the form teacher who levied appropriate sanctions depending on the offense.

The advent of the Basseterre Senior School was intended to provide the vast majority of students with an education beyond the Standard Seven Certificate which was the certification given at the end of an Elementary Education. This was a first step in the introduction of the Comprehensive Education System that was eventually fully implemented in 1966.

To get in the St. Kitts Nevis Grammar School or the Girls' High School; the only two public secondary schools on the island, one had to do well on the entrance and scholarship examinations. These examinations were held once per year. I had written these examinations twice before and was never successful to be selected to go to the St. Kitts Nevis Grammar School. Towards the end of 1961

I sat the entrance and scholarship examinations for the third time. At that period in our education history only twenty five to thirty boys and a similar number of girls were admitted to the Grammar School and Girls' High School respectively. To go to secondary school at that time one had to be brilliant or well connected. Many persons had to forego the opportunity of a secondary education, because their grades were not good enough to compete for the few scholarships that were available and even though they ranked high enough for paid entrance, many were unable to pay the school fees of sixteen dollars and eighty cents plus one dollar and twenty cents game fees for each term of about three months. The sum of eighteen dollars was beyond the affordability of the parents of the working class in an environment where domestic servants made less than one dollar per day and factory workers made ten to twenty dollars for a six day week. Field workers were even in a tighter financial straight jacket than factory workers.

When I wrote the examinations for a third time, there were two hundred and four boys packed into the auditorium of the Grammar School. I can remember Sir Probyn Inniss, then senior master of English of the school welcoming us to the exercise and encouraging us to do our best. He pointed out that how well we did would go a long way in determining how well we would do in our entire life. My desk was on the stage of the auditorium in the front row.

First up was Arithmetic, it could not have been better. I had seen everything before and it was if they had changed some of the numbers only to protect the integrity of the paper. I was certain that I had all available marks as I had time to work through the paper twice and only got reconfirmation on every answer, with all side work in place. We had a break then it was back for Intelligence Test and General Knowledge. That was good, and I completed the paper with time to do some revision. Lunchtime, it was the accustomed walk over the Ghaut and through Greenlands to get to Shaw Avenue for lunch. My Aunt Eunice was home to provide me with lunch and then she cheered me on and wished me good luck as I left for the afternoon session. The afternoon session was completely different from the morning secession. First up was English Composition and Comprehension. I struggled and completed most of the English papers and runs scored were from outside edges unlike the full blooded drives from the face centre of the bat of the early morning. The afternoon break was taken, Spelling and Dictation still to come. We settled back in the auditorium and the Dictation master stood on the steps leading to the stage and announced he was ready to start the dictation. Mr. R. J. Manchester, senior science master dictated the passage. The words 'energy' and 'enthusiasm' came frequently; they had me smothered. My greatest fear was realized. Mr. Manchester had a powerful voice as he had some experience in theatre in addition to which he was a Methodist lay preacher. His voice still reverberates in my head calling out 'energy' and 'enthusiasm'. The dreams of a secondary education were all shattered in the final session by my nemesis—Spelling and Dictation had done it again. It was a long wait for results.

When the application forms for the examinations were being filled, I told myself that I would not go back to take that exam. Almost all the boys from Mrs. Matilda Warner's 1A and several of the girls had their application forms endorsed by Mrs. Warmer. Realizing that there was no form with my name on it she called me and asked me why? My response was that I had taken the exams on two previous occasions and was unsuccessful and that I have decided that at age sixteen, I would get a job as an apprentice in either the electrical, mechanic or the machine shops at the Basseterre Sugar factory and work my way up to become an overseer or foreman. I was very familiar with the systems at the Sugar Factory as my father and godfathers worked there. Later that day, Mrs. Warner gave me an application form with her endorsement and signature. She instructed me to fill in the relevant parts of name, date of birth and so on and further instructed me to take it to my father for his endorsement. All that was done and my father was only too happy to do the endorsement for the promise to pay fees and other forms of support.

Nineteen sixty two (1962) was the centenary of the inception of the St. Kitts Nevis Grammar School. The government of the day with the Right Honourable Sir Robert L Bradshaw as the political leader of the Labour Movement and the Honourable C A P Southwell, Chief Minister and the Honourable Joseph N France, Minister of Social Services made a decision for an increase in the admission of pupils to the two government owned secondary schools to at least one hundred.

My name did not appear on the list after the first cut was published. I was seeing the day when I would have my own business, working as an electrician or mechanic. I knew that all was not lost because I knew men like Cecil "Buster" Walker and Lloyd 'Uncle Procs' Procope who had these successful businesses and they had not gone to Grammar School. It was the order to increase the number of intake that rescued me. On the interview with the principal of the Grammar School Mr. A. T. Ribeiro, my father and I, Mr. Ribeiro marvelled over the marks in Arithmetic as compared with the marks in Spelling and Dictation. I had scored a perfect century in Arithmetic and low twenties in spelling and dictation. That admission to the St. Kitts Nevis Grammar School changed the projected pathway of my life.

I went to my new school on January 4, 1962. I was the first member of my family, in all generations, to go to Grammar School.

CHAPTER 6

Extra-curricular at Basseterre Boys'

I was never selected for anything at Basseterre Boys. I never made a class team in track and field, cricket or football the popular sports played by the boys nor was I given the opportunity to represent the school in any national or public event. I never had the opportunity to go to Pond's Pasture like most of the boys from the Newtown area or to stay on at afternoons and weekends at Warner Park like the 'Park Rats' from The Ghaut, Dorset and other areas of Central Basseterre, to develop the skills and dexterity necessary in these sports. There was a National Spelling-Bee competition that featured all the government elementary schools and Basseterre Boys' had become famous for its record of success in these events and was always the school to beat. I can remember the year that two of my classmates were chosen on the Spelling-Bee team and they were eliminated at some point in the competition; the word that floored them became their nicknames for several years later; 'Sausage' and 'Balloon' know who they are. There was no mental arithmetic competition. Sausage went on to represent the national teams in track and field events as well as football (soccer) and Balloon went on to represent the national team in cricket.

One of my pastimes was sailing boats in the big drain that led from the western end of Lozac Road to Mr. Bias' shop on Pond Road. We made boats from popsicles sticks and cane peeling and were in and out of the drain channel to clear the boats when they got stuck on debris of various types. My boats always did well because I read somewhere that if the bottom of the boat was waxed with beeswax they would sail faster. This was true and it was not until years later that I understood the scientific principle behind this phenomenon. The wax reduced the friction on the boat caused by the surface tension of the water, thus increasing the speed, a secret that I kept from my friends. I had to be home at Roxborough Street by the sound off of the four o'clock hour by the Sugar Factory horn. After reaching home, it was something to eat, then the chores of washing bottles and the many other activities that were assigned to me as related to my mother's industry.

My friends, the other two CW's were able to join the Methodist group of the Lifeboys and the Boy's Brigade. I never had the opportunity to learn how to swim, go on hikes, and go on camps and other healthy activities that they enjoyed. My social standing in Basseterre Boy's was dependent on my strength in Arithmetic and the number of pennies that I could afford, to share in the goodies from the trays on the outside of the school during break time. I always had more than the other boys, for activities like fairs and garden parties. I was always there for those events. Those days, the average entrance to a fair was three pence (6 cents). My mother sometimes would give me as much as two shillings (48 cents) to attend these fairs. My favourite was the donkey cart ride. We paid six pence (12 cents) to the owner of the donkey cart for a ride around Taylors', the Sugar Factory and Warner's Park. Many of my friends enjoyed themselves by running along with the cart and slinging on every now and then, chancing a risk of being lashed with a whip from the driver of the donkey cart. They simply could not afford to pay for a ride.

At Basseterre Boys we had a savings club. We made deposits which were recorded on a card and at the end of the year we collected our accumulated amount. My mother gave me money every Monday morning to deposit. The first year I participated, my amount exceeded one hundred dollars, this was considered to be a sizable sum in those days. The headmaster instructed me to tell my mother to come for the money because it was too much for me to walk with. She sent me back with a message to the headmaster to say that she had no time to come to the school and that he should give me the money because it was I who brought every cent to the school. I received over one hundred dollars in an envelope and placed it in my pocket and ran continuously from Basseterre Boys' to our home on Roxborough Street.

Work and industry were hallmarks in our family. One year it was the time of the mango season in Monkey Hill, St. Peters and a number of persons from the Newtown area walked their way to Monkey Hill to buy mangoes from the owners of mango orchards to retail in Basseterre. Two women, Miss Aggie and Melvina were the group leaders. I joined that group of women and children in their venture starting from Newtown at about four o'clock in the morning. My mother gave me six pence to start my mango business. We got an average of seven long mangoes for a penny from the orchard owners and occasionally we hustled a few extras. We retailed mangoes at three for a penny thus making a one hundred percent profit with a margin of one mango for personal use. The trek from Monkey Hill to Roxborough Street was about three and a half miles and about one hour's walking. My profits were stored in an Andrew's Liver Salt can which had a sealed lid with a slot and every day I was able to deposit a six pence piece. My profits grew from this enterprise.

Another enterprise involved going to the salt ponds at Frigate Bay to pick salt. In the latter part of the long summer vacation, at a time when the ponds were crusted with salt, we walked to Frigate Bay to reap the salt. One had to wade into the pond, sometimes up to waist height. The salt was collected in buckets. The Frigate Bay Estate, then owned by the Wigley family was overseen by a Mr. Foster. For every two buckets of salt harvested one had to be deposited on a heap for the Estate, the other was kept by the harvester. I joined the Newtown crew that went to pick salt at Frigate Bay. The salt was rinsed with sea water to get rid of any residual mud. The salt was then dried in the open sunlight to remove any excess water. Salt was sold by the butter pans and my mother paid me the wholesale rate, the same as what she would pay other persons from whom she would buy.

Sea side grapes provided another source of income for entrepreneurs who went to Frigate Bay and Conaree to collect grapes from the trees that grew wild on the shoreline adjacent to the beaches. Sea grapes were sold in funnels that were made from sea grape leaves. The leaves were folded in a manner to form a cone, the form and size was maintained by pinning the leaves with a pointer from the coconut palm. Grapes were sold for a penny for a funnel.

Many of my evening hours were spent on the side road looking after and selling from a tray with the many commodities that were sold by my mother.

Gains from my enterprises and other adventures as well as gifts, were also deposited in my piggy bank. By Christmas when my bank was opened, I had a sum of money for my personal use, far in excess of any amount I ever had before.

In those days many of the neighbourhood children frequented our yard either to buy something for their parents or simply hang around hoping that my mother would find some task for them to do and hoping for a reward of some kind of goodies like sugar cake or some form of pudding. At times especially on Saturdays when my mother was out selling I was in control, and acted like a Czar, directing my playmates to do a number of chores which were left by my mother for me to do. There was always something that I could find to offer. For example, who washed the pot that the sugar cakes were made in had the right to scrape the residue and take it for them. During the cooking of black pudding, sometimes a link would burst and leave a considerable amount of the seasoned rice in the pot; this was a premium reward and the task commensurate with this type of reward could be something like sweeping the entire yard with a coconut broom. When my tasks were completed we resorted to a favourite pastime; playing 'dolly house' where we mimicked the extended family, depending on how many of us youngsters were available. Our house was raised about four feet from the ground level by concrete pillars.

This provided ample space for the activities of the extended family and we furnished the home with cardboard, crocus bags and boxes. Sometimes we played shop and we used the empty cans and boxes to represent the real items. The currency for the shop was cup-shell; these were bits of broken china ware that were salvaged from almost anywhere. Bits that had part of a decorative design had more value than others. There were marriages, and the ceremonies were accompanied with the full dramatization of priest and bridesmaid. The bride's train was made from the vines of the corolita plant, that grew wild everywhere and commonly called 'bee bush' and it was decorated with the pink blossoms of the same plant. The bouquet was usually made from crotons with the flower of a lily. It was not difficult to find lilies, because every household had at least two bunches planted on either side of the steps that lead to the main entrance of the homes. This was a local superstition; it was believed that the purity of the white lily prevented evil spirits from entering the home. I guess I was 'married' many a time on those occasions. In the dolly house culture I demanded the roles of the father and shop keeper.

I learnt one of life's greatest lessons during this period of life. Once I borrowed a rubber rat, that squeaked when squeezed, from one of our colleagues whom we called 'Red Roy' and somehow I could not find it to return to him. He cried for his prized possession and complained to his mother. That Saturday afternoon when my mother returned home from her first round of selling, his mother lodged their complaint. My mother asked me one question; whether I had borrowed the rat. I admitted and instantly it was a licking that I will never forget. After the blows I was sent into the bath to have a shower and put on some school clothes because she was taking me to town. In those days we had yard clothes, school clothes and church clothes. My mother literally dragged me from Roxborough Street, through George Street, through the Circus and then to The Bay Front where the Kawaja's had an open market type of business where they sold many items of hardware, household items and toys. This business was managed by a tall, fair woman, whom I knew very well, Mrs Lucina Clark. She had been a long time friend of my mother. I guess Mrs. Clark saw the rage on my mother's face and immediately enquired of her what she wanted. My mother described the rat to Mrs Clark, who picked up one and was coming back to the counter. My mother shouted to Mrs. Clark that she should bring two. My mother enquired of the price, it was six pence each, my mother opened her money bag and took out a shilling and hand it to me and said that I should pay the lady for the two rats. That shilling piece was mint new. We left the Bay Front, retraced our path to Roxborough Street and gave one of the rats to Red Roy and I was instructed that the other was for me. He was delighted with his brand new toy. That experience has lived with me. It taught me that whenever one borrows anything from another person one must be prepared to buy two, because one would need the use of the item another time. As fate would have it, I found the original rat sometime later and then I had two rubber rats. My mother then secured the new rat by locking it in her china cabinet and I never got it back until the next Christmas. I have always tried to acquire whatever I needed to use rather than borrowing. I hate to borrow and I do not like to lend.

It was one day during the Easter vacation that my mother left me a task of checking the completion of baking the last batch of cakes and pudding in the drum oven. She was rushed for time and left for the Sugar Factory. The classical check, beyond the visual, was to use a pointer from the leaf of the coconut palm. The pointer was inserted into the produce and removed. If the pointer came out without any mass on it, which indicated that the commodity was completely baked. I removed the fire from the oven, both internal and external. The external fire on the top of the drum oven was primarily a hefty piece of a tree limb, having removed it at the end of the baking; I placed it in the open yard and poured water on it as if to out it. I quickly secured the cakes and pudding as per my mother's instructions, had a bath and changed my yard clothing for more suitable school clothing to go to the Sugar Factory to join my mother.

I loved being at the Sugar Factory. The noise of the machinery, the heavy smoke rising from the chimneys, the sprays from the aeration of the waters of the cooling pond and the arrival of the locomotives with long train of carriages loaded with sugar cane and counting the carriages was so exciting. Another favourite thing for me to do was to be looking through the machine shop ventilation from the Breakfast Shed at the machinists working on lathes and grinders. The sparks from the grinding process showered to many places and it was as if I was looking at the Starlight that many of my friends only saw around Guy Fawkes and Christmas. That day at the end of business at the Sugar Factory, my mother and her entourage returned to our home at Roxborough Street. My mother got home before I did. As I came within her sight from around the north-eastern corner of the main house, she hurled a one gallon paint pan at me. I ducked but did not go down low enough. The pan landed on the crown of my head and opened a wound in my scalp. I ran away only to realize that I was being washed in blood, I ran to the top of Roxborough Street. I was helped by Mr. Bias' daughter Collie. She took me to the back of their shop and administered the necessary first aid to arrest the bleeding and eventually she shaved the area and applied a dressing which she secured with sticking plaster—Elastoplasts. I never returned to my mother's house, instead I went to my grandmother's—Narna.

It was about the dusk of that evening that my mother came to collect me. There it was a rage of words from my grandmother who was threatening to call the police for my mother. My mother's only response was that she had come to collect her child. She sat on the steps until my grandmother sent me out. My mother hugged me and said that she was sorry, but I must be more careful. What had caused all this was that the tree limb that I had removed from the oven was not sufficiently saturated with water and the heat from within caused it to smoulder and eventually rekindle. The only thought in my mother's mind at that time was that my carelessness might have caused her to lose her most valued material possession, her wooden house. That was the lesson; that one should never put out a fire in a hurry.

My glory days were occasions like Easter and Christmas when the Sunday schools had their concerts. By age seven I went to three

Sunday schools. At two o'clock it was Hope Chapel the Methodist organization on George Street. From three to four o'clock it was Mrs. White's Sunday school. They were affiliated to the Ebenezer Church of God on Central Street. And then from four thirty to six it was Mrs. Richardson's Sunday school, which was affiliated with the Zion Moravian Church. This meant that I had to remember three golden texts that I had to recite to my mother when I got home. Many days I substituted some standard ones that I kept in my arsenal. The benefits for me were that I got the opportunity to go on three Sunday school picnics every year. I was always given poems to recite—recitations—in every Sunday school. My mother beamed with glory on the many occasions when I was called for an encore. She always came to hear me recite. She was my coach and director. The lyrics were drummed into me with lashes that forced me to absorb the contents and deliver a rendition with flourish and style. I can remember one year I was given one of the recitations from the senior class. It was long and difficult. On Holy Thursday night I did not get it in to my mother's satisfaction, and I got a myriad of lashes with a leather sandal. I guess she was either exhausted or sorry for me as after a long session, I was sent to bed. The tradition was that on Good Friday we went to Ponds Pasture to fly kites. I had my kite already, one well made by custom order. I was ready to leave home, having swept the yard and ate my breakfast; I was ready to leave for Pond's Pasture. My mother said that I should put down the kite and bring the recitation to her. It was the ultimate rehearsal; by the time I was up to par it was midday. I never got to fly my custom made kite until after lunch. Easter Sunday afternoon was the time for the concert at Hope Chapel. I was the first to recite in the second half of the program. My rendition was outstanding and the calls for encore went out, I repeated my oration with equal style and confidence. It was the moment that my mother had laboured with me for over that weekend. The praise and commendations came in torrents.

I was about eleven years old when I awoke one morning and saw my mother smiling with something like a postcard in her hand reading. The smile was brilliant, nothing less than the glowing radiance of the midday sun, I asked what it was. She said to me that it was an invitation to a wedding. I enquired whose wedding. My mother patted her chest and said that it was her wedding. I was so surprised. Previously I had heard my mother boast and say that she did not want to get married because she was an independent woman who could look after herself. From that day I knew that I should not take any woman seriously when she makes a statement to say that she does not want to get married. My parents got married on Saturday, November 29, 1958 at the Roman Catholic Church on East Square Street. The wedding was at four o'clock in the afternoon and the reception was held at the Mutual Improvement (MIS) Hall on Market Street. My mother received several gifts for her wedding, especially from the many persons whom she had assisted in some way to go to England. The biggest contributor was Bertram 'Bertie' Browne one of her adopted wards.

Bertie left St. Kitts at the age of nineteen to go to England. After leaving the Basseterre Boys' he worked as an apprentice at the Basseterre Sugar Factory's carpenter shop and he was the son of Mr. Daniel 'Big Dan' Browne. After the death of my brother Calvin, Bertie became the big brother of our family. Berite sent my mother her shoes, matching accessories of necklace, bangles and bracelets all in the hue and metal of silver. He also sent many yards of white lace and satin with which to make her dress. He sent her an eight place set of stainless steel cutlery with all the various implements all stacked in a brown leather case lined with red velvet.

My mother's wedding dress was made by my godmother Iris Crossman. Godmother Iris was a seamstress of national recognition. As was said in those days, she had turned out many brides of note before. Like my mother, my godmother was a pillar of iconic standing in the Newtown society.

The marriage of my parents was the terminal point of our years in Newtown. We then moved to #30 Shaw Avenue in McKnight.

CHAPTER 7

Shaw Avenue, McKnight

My father owned the house he lived in at Shaw Avenue and he lived as a bachelor with many visiting friends. He had several girl friends and many had children for him. My informers told me that there was a Glaslyn who bore his first two children Basil and Hyacinth, Maisey who had Sheila, and Ivy had Mildred aka Therese. These were all older than I was. My younger sister Yvette and I were the offspring of Lucille and then there is the last of my father's children, Aurille by Lillian; twenty one years my junior. There were many other girlfriends who never had children for him.

My father did a major reconstruction to his house at Shaw Avenue. The wooden house he had was reinforce so that it could withstand the pressures of lifting it about nine feet above the ground level. They used a number of screw jacks to lift the house and as the incremental gains in height were observed, there were props of wooden blocks and oil drums used to stabilized the house. When the desired height was attained and the levelling processes were completed a number of concrete columns were cast up to the main beams that supported the original house. The lower level was then filled in with the appropriate footings for the foundation, the flooring and eventually the side and partitioning walls with concrete blocks. On completion, my father had an upstairs edifice that consisted of three bed rooms, a large living room area, a veranda, and bath and toilet at the upper level, with an internal stairway which led down to the lower level. The ground floor had facility for a shop, opening directly to Shaw Avenue, with an adjacent room that was used as a recreational area for patrons of the shop. Next to the recreational room was another that was used as the family dining area and there was the kitchen. This was the dream of my father, a facility with both residential and commercial capacities. At the age of forty eight he was ready to settle down and chose my mother to be his bride.

My mother, my sister Yvette and I journeyed to our new home. The house at Roxborough Street was rented. I was still at Basseterre Boys and my journey to school took me through Greenlands, over Westbourne Ghaut, through Soho Village, through Ann Carr Alley and over the high steps, over the wall of College Street Ghaut, past the Wesley Methodist Church on Seaton Street and then to my *alma mater*. Life in Mc Knight was completely different. We now lived in an upstairs house, literally a level above the ordinary people and we had a shop.

The shop had two distinct divisions, even though there were no physical dividing boundaries, it was clear that the area to the north was the place for food stuff and other provisions and the area to the south was the place for the stronger and more stimulating stuff such as liquors. Mr Samuel Bias was the sponsor of my parents' application for a liquor license and he provided all the goods required for the stocking of the shop. The initial stock in November of 1958 was just in excess of two thousand Eastern Caribbean dollars. My parents made a deposit of eight hundred dollars, information which I gathered from the shop book, and they made payments and credited other stuff as they were needed. I was the point man to take orders and made the payments to Mr Bias shop.

My mother was transformed from husker to shopkeeper and she tended the shop from as early as six thirty in the morning to maybe ten in the late evening. We sold almost everything; from the basic staples of rice, flour and cornmeal to frozen chicken parts in the provision section to the basic white cask rum to beer and stout to whiskey and vermouth. The business flourished and within the first year of operations the deficit with Mr Bias was wiped off. My sister Sheila joined my mother in the shop as her principal helper.

In those days every rum shop had a name. There were the famous "London House" and "Satellite Bar" of Irish Town and the "Ajax" of Newtown. My father toyed with a name for his business. One day he was painting a sign board with a name, when one of his friends and patron of the bar suggested that the shop should be called "Dodge City". He immediately scrapped his idea and got another of his friends to do, in professional graphics, the sign that he eventually hung atop the entrance to the business place. To this day in 2012, after many different changes of businesses at #30 Shaw Avenue, My sister Yvette runs a business, very similar to the one that my parents started in 1958, under the name of "Dodge City".

My tasks became less laborious but the time and hours were still demanding. By the time I got home from school I had to be in the shop to give my mother some relief. My routine job was to weigh out the staples in one and two pound paper bags, fold them shut and stack them in appropriate heaps for easy dispensing. My father had two dogs and a number of chickens. It was my job at mornings to clean the post digestive discharge of both dogs and chickens. Over two-thirds of the yard area was covered with concrete as well as the flooring of the fowl house. That made it easy to wash away the filth with a jet of water from a hose connected to a delivery tap, while brushing with a bass broom. Then it was time to provide the food to both chickens and dogs that will provide the digestive discharge for my job next day.

I never got the time to go and play cricket and football with the other boys at Greenlands pasture or the playing field at the Gardens on a regular basis. On Sundays, the shop was officially closed, and my father took care of the stragglers who came by to purchase liquor. On Sunday mornings I went to Wesley Methodist church for the nine o'clock service and then went back at two o'clock in the afternoon for Sunday school. After Sunday school it was the event of the week, a lime that took one through the Circus, down to the treasury pier, and all the way to the War Memorial. We played and heckled each other; it was the occasion when one might have an opportunity to

47

talk to members of the opposite sex. In later years the Ritz Cinema, operated by John Eid of the Eid Brothers of Lebanese origin, ran matinees from four-thirty on Sunday afternoons. This provided alternative recreation for those who could afford the entrance fees. I saw many movies at Ritz, those that come to mind include "To Hell and Back" and "Drums Across the River"—starring Audy Murphy, "Purple Mask"—starring Tony Curtis. I went to the Ritz Cinema almost every Sunday afternoon.

My free time on Sundays after church was spent at Irish Town Bay, enjoying the surf as it lapped against the body and the adventure of going out as far as one could stand and then diving back towards the shore. It was a common assault for the bigger boys to hold the younger ones and duck them under the water for several times. It was at Irish Town Bay that I eventually learnt how to swim. As one developed ones swimming there were targets that one had to be able to attain; Church Tower: to be out far enough to tell the time from the St. Georges Anglican Church clock, Milliken: to be able to see the chimney stack at Milliken Estate and Steamer Mark: the area where the inter island vessels anchored within the Basseterre Harbour. I never made it to Steamer Mark. Some Sundays we would walk up to the Treasury Pier, jump off, and swim parallel to the shoreline until we were back at Irish Town.

At the back of the shop in Shaw Avenue, in the recreational room, there was a jukebox that provided music as part of the entertainment for the patrons. Songs of various types were on the records that composed the selections on the jukebox. Artists like Lord Kitchener, Lord Melody and the Mighty Sparrow of Trinidad provided the latest in calypsos and the sentimental love songs of Bing Crosby and Frank Sinatra were part of the selections. The patrons, both men and women, would punch selections of their choice and danced to the music. It was an average of five cents for a tune. There was a lot of merry making, especially on Friday and Saturday evenings when most of the working class people got paid.

It was a Friday evening when there was a confrontation between my mother and my father. My understanding was that one of my father's old girl friends was at the shop and she and my father might have been very familiar with each other. I guess that evoked some jealousy from my mother. Later that night after the shop was closed there was a heated argument between my parents. A fight broke out and after some exchange of blows, my mother took me by the hand and dragged me down stairs to the street and we proceeded back to Newtown to my grandmother's house. We spent the night there. My younger sister Yvette was already asleep so we left her in her bed. Early next morning on the rise of the sun, my father was knocking on my grandmother's door. He apologised profusely and invited my mother and me to come back to Mc Knight. We went back after breakfast. I had never heard an argument between my parents before or after that occasion.

In November of 1959 my mother took ill and had to be taken to the Cunningham Hospital. She had surgery and shortly thereafter she developed pneumonia and succumbed to the fever. My mother died before her first wedding anniversary by six days. This was traumatic for me at eleven years old and my younger sister Yvette, who at that time was only four.

My sister Sheila took charge of the shop and the domestic affairs of the household. By then Sheila had her first two children Keith and Seymour. Keith was a toddler and Seymour was an infant. Sheila never took up fulltime residence with us at Shaw Avenue but returned to her home in Irish Town where she continued to live with her mother and several other siblings. We had for the first time, the employment of a fulltime domestic assistant.

There were several domestic assistants at different points in time. They came and left that job for many different reasons. I remembered one who took her holiday pay to make up her passage to go to St. Thomas, US Virgin Islands, where she resided for over forty years, raised her family there and they all became US Citizens. She has since retired from her labours in the USVI and has returned to her native village and built a big dream house, where she intend to spend the evenings of her years amongst her extended family, while enjoying the financial rewards of a pension and Social Security from the United States Federal Government. The most outstanding of our domestic assistants was a woman named Ivy Edwards. She worked with our family for several years, before she left us for a more lucrative job; making pastries in a bakery in Basseterre. She helped raise me and my sister Yvette.

Sometime after my mother's death my father invited my cousin Esmond to come to St. Kitts from Nevis to live with us at Shaw Avenue. He was then a teenager who had completed his elementary education at St. Thomas' School on Nevis and had attained the Seven Standard Certification. His job was to be the shop keeping assistant to Sheila. We all got along for a while. Sheila was the first to leave the business. I never bothered to find out a reason for her departure. Esmond carried the weight of the business for a while before my father invited his sister Aunt Eunice to come from Curacao, one of the ABC Islands in the Dutch Antilles. It was about the time when there was a lot of retrenchment taking place in the oil refining operations on that Island, when a number of the manual operations became automated.

Aunt Eunice came home and took charge of everything, business operations, domestic affairs and the raising of my sister Yvette and me. She was our de facto mother. She cared for us and we never missed the love and affection, the security and the guidance that all youngsters needed, especially in those formative years. She had no children of her own. She embraced Yvette and me as if we were issues from her own body. We lacked nothing. She left her husband Edwin Henville, a native of St. Vincent and the Grenadines, back in Curacao. He made annual visits to St. Kitts. He was fortunate that he was retained at the oil refinery for a much longer period than he thought he would have been. They had bought a property at

Walwyn Avenue, Buckley's Site sometime earlier as part of their early retirement plan.

When my Aunt Eunice came to live with us at Shaw Avenue, she added a new dimension to the business. She brought a number of male and female garments from Curacao and displayed them by hanging them from the ceiling of the shop, still covered in transparent plastic. I can remember the fashionable plaid shirts and straight foot trousers that the men bought. Re-orders were made by way of her husband. The business continued to thrive.

My aunt was an exquisite dresser. When her wardrobe arrived from Curacao; I could remember counting over fifty pairs of shoes that were her personal belongings. She always wore the fashionable silk head ties that had come to be associated with the women who had returned from Curacao. She glided with confidence as she moved about in the shop or walked to the city to transact business. Aunt Eunice was heaven sent.

Some six years after taking over the business, she and my father had a major falling out. The business by then had begun to fade. Stocks had been depleted and eventually dwindled down to almost nothing. Poor management and excessive crediting to the families from the area must have been the main cause for the failure of the business. She left Shaw Avenue and went to her house at Walwyn Avenue, Trafalgar in the Village. Shortly thereafter she migrated to St. Croix, US Virgin Island. We continued to communicate by way of letters and gift parcels with goods for Yvette and me. There were times when I got some US dollars by mail or hand delivery by her friends as they came to St. Kitts from St. Croix.

CHAPTER 8

Social Life In Mc Knight

In Mc Knight the quality of life was apparently a little better than it was in Newtown. There were wide paved streets of Cunningham Street, Fort Thomas Road, Central Street, Burdon Street, Shaw, Thibou, Fiennes, Malone and Durant Avenues. The building of the infrastructure of the Mc Knight area was done as a planned project on the town expansion. The original city of Basseterre ended at Westbourne Ghaut. The lands west of Westbourne Ghaut were principally a cotton growing estate. These lands were owned by a Scottish family and were eventually earmarked for the urban development. The streets and alleyways were well laid out and the area was divided into house lots that were leased or rented to persons to build their houses. Our house at Shaw Avenue was on the extreme north western corner of the Mc Knight estate. At the time when we moved to Mc Knight the attorney for the Estate was Mr. William V. Herbert Sr. He collected the rent and wrote in a receipt book as attorney for Alma Brown. The lands were eventually offered for sale to the people whose houses occupied them.

Our home at Shaw Avenue had a WC connected to a septic tank system unlike the bore-hole privy which we had in Newtown. We had an internal bath and internal plumbing to the kitchen. We continued to enjoy a better quality of life than many of the others in our community. We had a deep-freezer for the shop and a standing refrigerator primarily for the family use.

The youths of Mc Knight hiked a lot. Trips to the mountains were part of our regular activity. We went to the areas of Milliken, Fountain and Sofa Stone looking for the wild fruits that grew there in abundance. The summer vacation was the time when we had our best exploits. Dates were a prime product. We threw stones high up into bunches of dates at the lower section of the crown of the date palm. Successful shots would result in a shower of dates falling to the ground which were then collected. Mangoes of many varieties were also sought. We climbed trees and handpicked ripened and full fruits. Cashews were also part of our exploits. The cashew had two valuable parts; the succulent part of the fruit was eaten directly or stewed in a syrup of sugar and cinnamon. The nuts were secured and dried in the sun for a period of time before they were roasted. The dried nuts were taken to areas outside of the city where they were roasted; the roasting of cashew nuts seemed to have had an adverse effect on chickens. Sugar cane was everyone's favourite. We went to the fields and cut our own canes, whether it was in or out of the time of the official harvesting. During the harvesting we went to the railway lines, climbed onto the carriages of the locomotives and pulled from the previously harvested sugar canes on their way to the Sugar Factory. The taking of sugar canes whether from the fields or the locomotives was illegal. The sugar factory had a number of security men, whom we called watchmen, and they were always in attendance. Many days we had to run to get away from the pursuit of the watchmen. Anyone who was caught was taken to the police station, and one's parents or guardian would have had to go to rescue them. Persons were sometimes charged with offenses for possession of sugar cane or trespassing on private property and had to make an appearance before the magistrate courts. Another and most dangerous act which we as youngsters committed was to hop on the locomotive and go for a joy ride. One had to learn the art of moving from one carriage to another while the train was in full motion. My first train ride was had right here on St. Kitts; I hopped onto a train at the Shadwell packing station on a west bound train. I was advised by more experienced crew that we would ride down west to the Du Port Packing Station just outside of West Farm Estate and when the train started to slow down we would jump from the train. It seems as if the train driver was anticipating our action, instead of slowing, he maintained the speed. I heard the order "jump" and saw the other guys from Mc Knight jumped from the train so I followed; my landing was far from perfect. I struggled to regain my balance by running but fell forward, belly first, and continued to roll down an incline away from the train; I ended up in a bed of sand and a patch of thistle plants with leaves that had small thorns on the tips of a serrated leaf. It was more embarrassing than painful; my first jump was a failure. On the return journey my jump was more successful as I was coached by some of my more experienced friends.

I can remember on one occasion a Mc Knighter, also known as 'de Doll', lost one of his legs while attempting to pull sugar cane from a moving train. Somehow he got entangled and was dragged by the train until one of his legs was crushed between the metallic wheels and rail of the train. His leg had to be amputated. This never deterred us, but encouraged us to be more careful and cautious.

On one Public Holiday a party of about fifteen of us decided to hike the entire length of the South Eastern Peninsular. We congregated at Miss. Ann's steps. Our appointed time of departure was to be three o'clock in the morning. When we had our party together we departed and by the time we reached the Basseterre Police Station the big clock on the walls inside the Guard Room was saying 3:00 am. We continued our journey along Pond Road, through to the Frigate Bay Road and up Timothy Hill by way of an unpaved track, wide enough for four wheel drive jeeps that were used by the owners and residents of Friars Bay and the Salt Pond areas. The Jeep track continued over to Majors Bay with a fork diverting to Cockleshell Bay and Mosquito Bay (now called Turtle Beach). By 6:00 am we were over at the Great Salt Pond and witnessed the majesty of the sunrise with the varying hues of dawn changing from black to crimson, to red, to orange, and then yellow and eventually to the blazing silvery white of early morning. We circumvented the pond and went down to Majors Bay. We all had food and water and when we got to Major's Bay we rested and had breakfast. I had corned beef, to which the sand flies seemed to take a particular liking. Fortunately, the sand flies had no bones in them.

After breakfast we explored the entire area of Major's Bay. We took to the rocks and collected whelks. Some of the guys had fishing lines, but none of them caught anything of note. I had a substantial amount of whelks and had to tie them in my outer shirt and onto the end of a stick which I carried over my shoulder. The return march was tiring in the heat of the blazing mid-morning and noon day sun. We were back in Frigate Bay by one o'clock. We joined in with the many picnic makers at Frigate Bay where most of us swam after having lunch. I was too tired at the end of the day to walk back to Mc. Knight; I hopped a ride on the deck of an open truck that took me back to Shaw Avenue, definitely exhausted.

Another fun thing was to take fruits from trees without the authorization of the owner. We built pyramids and human ladders to get the necessary height and elevation for fruits that hung close to the fences. Greenlands was our area of greatest exploitation. I can remember an event when Ashton "Dabrio" Maynard and I formed the base; Kendall "Chigi-dick" Somersall formed the second tier and Emrod "Swallow" Martin climbed onto the shoulders of "Chigi-dick" to reach a branch with genips or skinip as we called them. Emrod got up in fine style and started to pick the genips, handing them down to Kendal and then to Ashton or me depending on which hand he was using. The pressure got a bit too much for Ashton and he collapsed and three of us came to the ground, leaving Emrod hanging to the branches of the tree maybe eight to ten feet from the ground. He was in a dilemma dangling from the branches; should he let go the branches and fall back to the street or pull himself up into the tree and climb-down the trunk. The latter would have been disastrous because a bad dog was already on the alert in the yard. Emrod decided to jump and he landed safely on his feet. We took our bounty for that evening and went to Greenlands Pasture to enjoy our feast of genips.

Cricket was our major sporting activity. The boys from the upper section of Mc Knight played on Greenland's Park, at afternoons, weekends and every day during the vacation periods. We made our own balls from used bicycle inner tubes. The tubes were cut in transverse strips about three-eighths of an inch wide. The rubber bands, thus produced, were woven onto a core, that was a mocker seed or a large marble, to make a ball that was built up to a size of about two and a half inches in diameter and about the weight of the standard cricket ball. This type of ball had to be a Kittitian invention, as I had never seen this type of ball in any other place in the region or further afield.

Bats were made from the limbs of trees by flattening one side of the circular piece of a branch of the appropriate length and width and the handle carved at one end to a comfortable grip. Our master bat maker was my next door neighbour Rembrandt Knight whom we also called by his grandfather's name Peter Harvey. On the north-eastern boundary point between my father's property and the land owned by the original Peter Harvey was a great calabash tree. The calabash tree produced a strong and relatively light wood, which we often called "Cup-wood" and this was used for making cricket bats. Rembrandt had access to some of his grandfather's carpentry tools and would have learnt some of his carpentry skills from his grandfather. The bats he took time to make looked like those that were purchased from the sports stores in town.

More commonly used for bats was the lower portion of the stem of a coconut branch and a handle carved at the tapered end. We also went on construction sites to search for thick pieces of wood that were strong enough to withstand the shock from the rubber ball. A piece of rough pitch pine 2 x 4 of the appropriate length was the ideal find. We trimmed the thick pieces of board to the appropriate size with machetes and other implements to provide an improvised bat. It was like winning the grand prize when we acquired a used bat from an established cricketer.

The boys from the lower section of Mc Knight played cricket at the Gardens. Challenges between upper and lower Mc Knight were usually played on neutral grounds at the Springfield Pasture. The northern wall of the fence of the Governors' mansion was used as a pavilion under the shade of the Sand-way Pine trees that lined the boundary of the Governor's property. Even though I was never good enough to make a first team I was always around. We played challenges from other districts such as Village and Newtown.

There are two incidents that occurred while we were playing cricket at Greenlands that stand out in my memory. One day during the summer vacation we were playing a pick up match, Bertram "Tramming" Mc Mahon vs. Vincent "Hardy" Hendrickson. They were the captains of the respective teams. "Tramming's" team scored a considerable total. "Hardy" in his determined effort to overtake the total posted by his opponents, hooked a ball bowled to him into a window pane of one of the houses on the eastern side of Park Lane, Greenlands. The ball crashed the window pane and sent pieces of glass all over, inside and outside of the house. Our initial reaction was to run, but later we returned to apologise and promised to replace the louver window pane of glass. We measured the dimensions and went downtown to A.M. Losada Ltd hardware store to find out the cost. We searched our pockets for all the pennies we could muster. It took us the better part of the day for us begging around the city to raise two dollars and ninety five cents that was required to purchase the replacement glass. We went back to the home and apologised to the owner, who was gracious enough to do the actual replacement for us.

The other incident happened when I was not playing at Greenlands. I was trapped in the shop helping to parcel out the basic staples in paper bags. There was an early session on Greenlands. "Sam" Condor came into our shop at Shaw Avenue limping. His story was that he intended to play an on-drive while he was batting in a get-a-ball—bowl session of cricket but instead of hitting the ball he played his big toe on the left foot. He was in a lot of pain as he hobbled his way from Greenland's Park to our shop. "Sam" requested that I should follow him to the Cunningham Hospital which was only one street away. We started walking down Shaw Avenue then across Thompson Street then on to Burdon Street. By the time we got to the hospital gate his left foot was swollen to a frightening size and he could hardly walk anymore. I took "Sam" on my back and made our way to the emergency/outpatient division of the hospital. We met a senior nurse who was the first to examine his foot. Sometime later a doctor came and examined his foot a second time. The doctor determined that the joint that connected the toe to the foot was dislocated and by manipulating the toe by pushing and pulling on it, he was able to set it back in position. The doctor eventually bandaged the foot and toes with a wooden splint in place, and gave "Sam" some ACP tablets which he had to take with food, to manage the pain. While at the hospital I was reprimanded by the nurse, she cautioned me of my carelessness to be allowing the younger ones to be playing without supervision. I took the reprimand in style and did not make her any wiser of the age difference between "Sam" and me in spite of the difference in physical size. The fun started when we got back to "Sam's" home. By then his mother had reached home and found that the yard was not swept, the dishes were not washed the chores that she had assigned to him were incomplete. In spite of the bandage on his foot and my explanation of the events that had transpired that morning his mother Bernice "Bern" Bridgwater place a solid cut tail on "Sam".

"Sam" had hoped that he would have been able to get in an early bit of cricket and get back home to complete his chores before his mother got back from the market. In those days, very few things could have spared one from the rod of correction.

Many of my friends in Mc Knight sought to find various types of jobs to help them to provide some much needed income, so that they could contribute to their household's budget or to get some of the toys and other goods that they wanted. My friends worked as gardeners and household attendants for many of the families in the upper echelons of society such as the European and Asian descendants that lived at Fortlands. Some worked as newsboys selling and distributing the local newspapers such as the Daily Bulletin and the Labour Spokesman. Fortunately for me I had readymade employment at our shop; and my Aunt Eunice or my father provided most of my needs. It was not too difficult for me to subsidise my allowances with cash from the drawer of the shop but I wanted to experience some of the difficulties that some of my friends had to endure.

My first employment outside our family operation came in the summer vacation of 1964. Roy "Gloochy" Roper introduced us to the day Labour system of the St. Kitts Breweries at Buckley's. The custom was that on days when the brewery was bottling their products they took on extra day-labour workers. Three of us from the Mc Knight area, "Gloochy", Emrod and I decided to go to the brewery with the hope of getting picked for day-labour. The first morning we went to the brewery they had put off the picking of day labourers until the next day.

As we left the brewery, heading back to Mc Knight, we met our friend Gilbert "Mountbatten" Thompson heading to a place called Broomay on Olivees Mountain where his family farmed a sizable acreage of land by growing ground provisions and raising animals. We decided to go to Broomay with Gilbert. We walked all the way, while Gilbert rode on his donkey. The journey was not difficult for us. We enjoyed the wild fruits of cashew, guava and fat-pork on route. By the time we got to the farm area, Gilbert's father Willie Thompson was there hours earlier to milk the cows. Gilbert joined in and helped his father with the milking. We explored the area within the close proximity of the farm. We were in excess of one thousand feet above sea level, and the moisture and dew of the early mornings supported the growth of everything. At the higher elevation we found raspberries growing in abundance on the fringes of the rainforest. Raspberries were in season, and we consumed as much as we could and at the same time collecting some to take back home with us.

We left Broomay with Gilbert taking two pans with milk, containing in excess of five gallons, cradled in the crooks, on his donkey. By the time we got back to Olivees Estate yard Gilbert's mother was there to collect the milk. Sarah Thompson was a tall strong woman. It was customary for her to take both pans with milk, one on her head and the other in her hand, and carry them from Olivees Estate back to Shaw Avenue in Mc Knight. That morning Mrs Thompson took one pan comfortably on her head and the three of us, taking turns struggled with the other in an effort to help her.

By the time we reached Greenlands she started to distribute the milk. As she got to the customers' gate she called out the family name in a very familiar manner that served both as a greeting and a call for them to collect the milk. Someone from the household would emerge with one or two clean bottles to collect their milk. Mrs. Thompson took the pan from her head opened it and with an enamel cup filled the bottles with milk and returned them to the customer. We made about four stops in Greenlands before we got back to Mc Knight. I got back home at Shaw Avenue and started my routine chores for the day; I had no concerns for breakfast as we had consumed quantities of wild fruits on our adventure to Broomay.

The next day, the three of us were up early and we journeyed to the brewery. We waited for the manager to come to pick the day labourers. The Manager was a white Englishman named Craig. We stood in line as he selected. "You and you" he said as he pointed to different persons. I got the penultimate pick leaving Emrod and one other person in line. The manager selected the other person leaving Emrod as the sole reject. We went into the plant, first to a shed area where we were given rubber boots as a means of protection so as to reduce the chances of slipping on the wet concrete floors of the plant.

My first task at the brewery was to clean dust from the riggings that supported a silo in which grain was stored inside the plant. The

60

painted metal structure was covered with dust in layers up to one sixteenth of an inch thick. The tools provided were a four inch paint brush and several yard of dusting cloth. I did the initial dusting with the paint brush and then polished away the remaining dust with the dusting cloth. It took me until eleven o'clock that morning to complete my first assigned task. I was then sent for lunch. This was the time I faced my greatest dilemma. I had no money to buy lunch from one of the shops in the vicinity of the plant, so I had to rush home to Mc Knight.

As I walked home I was deciding what strategy I would use to tell my father about the day job at the brewery. Several thoughts went through my head. By the time I got home my father was in the shop and he was furious that he had not seen me for the morning and he did not know of my whereabouts. As I approached the shop the dreaded question came. My response was that a number of us decided to go for an early morning walk and as we passed by the brewery, the manager was selecting persons to do day work at the plant and the other boys decided that they would join the line to see if they would get pick for the job and so I went in too. I got picked for two days to work at the brewery. My father accepted my explanation wholesale, to my greatest relief. I had lunch and returned to the brewery for my afternoon stint.

When I got back to the brewery I reported to the plant engineer, Cromwell Ira Bowry a gentleman whom I knew very well. He took me to the bottling hall where they were bottling Giant Malt. Mr Bowry introduced me to Mr. Hicks who was the foreman of the bottling hall. My first task in the bottling hall was to use a trolley to take cases of dirty bottles from a stack to the washing machine. I took about twenty cases of empty bottles per trip on the broad based trolley and stacked them within the reach of the operators who were loading the washing machine. Twelve bottles were stacked in a row on the deck adjacent to the entry port. By pushing a lever each batch of bottles were taken into the machine; as jets automatically fitted into the mouth of the bottles and they went through the machine for different phases of the wash. The washing phases included boiling in hot caustic soda (sodium hydroxide) solution and other detergents where high pressure jets washed both inside and outside the bottles. They were finally washed and rinsed with cold water and dried with hot air before they emerged at the other end of the machine ready for the bottling line. The bottler moved in clockwise rotation as the synchronized belts, lifters and jets went through the paces of filling with the product and capping the individual bottles. As the capped product emerged from the filler they were allowed to accumulate on a table before the next phase. The products were later stacked onto stainless steel carts with perforated trays and then placed in pasteurizers for about forty minutes where the product was pasteurized by heating and cooling at sustained temperatures to reduce the bacterial content of the product so as to give them longer shelf life. After pasteurizing, the products were removed from the stainless steel carts and stacked into empty cases. The final stage was labelling, which was done by a machine with each individual bottle loaded onto the labeller manually.

It was really exciting for me to have worked at the brewery; I saw the application of many of the scientific principles that I had to learn in school, in meaningful and practical applications.

It was prohibited to drink any of the produce when they were being bottled, but we found ways and means to short circuit the prohibition. I saw my colleagues drinking and in a short period I caught on to the trick of getting ice cold malt to drink. I guess I had four or five malts on my first afternoon in the bottling hall. The next day my task in the bottling hall was the same. I completed my first two days as a day labourer at the St. Kitts Brewery Limited at a pay rate of three dollars ($3.00) Eastern Caribbean Currency per day. At the end of day two I collected my first ever pay envelope with six dollars.

When I got home from work I told my father that I had gotten six dollars pay for the two days and attempted to offer him some money. I got the rebuff of my life. He said that he did not send me to work, I chose to go to work, which was a good thing and that the money was mine to keep; he further stated that he would not live long enough to become dependent on any of his children for their money. The later part of the statement has lived deep within me for all these years. I am hopeful that I would be able to make that said remark to my children with a fair amount of certainty.

I went to the brewery for day jobs for about three years during the Easter and summer vacations.

The youths of Mc Knight gathered at evenings on Thibou Avenue outside the shop and home of a lady who was called Miss Ann. Miss Ann was a Montserratian and she was believed to have mystic powers and to be able to perform a number of super human acts. We feared her but the street lamp and her steps were the focus of our meeting place. We talked everything on Miss Ann's steps and humoured and heckled each other about any and everything. It was a place where we spent most of our evening hours while we were within the Mc Knight community. Some nights we walked in groups of up to twenty strong, on our way to the Apollo Cinema or just for a simple stroll through the city.

The most influential of the boys from Mc Knight was Paul "Jocko" Thomas. He was the chief heckler as well as the leader of most of the mischievous acts in which the boys of Mc Knight involved themselves. He had many aliases amongst them were "De Cock" and "Pliers Foot". The later was derived from the very pronounced bow legs which he had. He was clever; he climbed trees with such ease and agility that made one think that he was a member of the ape family. "Jocko" as he was most affectionately called, was not able to run very fast but because of his bow legs he had a relatively low centre of gravity which gave him extra stability in dodging. I can remember once a number of us were being chased from the railway track with sugar canes by a watchman. The watchman purposely targeted "Jocko". The watchman was getting closer and closer to "Jocko". "Jocko" tacked through a pigeon peas patch on Greenland and held on to a limb of a pigeon peas tree and with perfect timing he let go the limb which flicked back from its stressed position to hit the watchman flush in his face. That knocked the watchman flat on his back thus giving us enough time to escape. "Jocko" went on to play football (soccer) as goal-keeper for the St. Kitts National Team for many years until he migrated to the US Virgin Islands.

Dominoes were a big part of our evening's activities. One place where we played was under a streetlamp outside the home of the Thompsons. Willie and Sarah were the home owners. They had two sons and a grandson who played dominoes with us. We played the game of partners for one hundred chalks. We were ridiculed if our opponents reached 100 chalks before we got to 25 counts that would result in a name that is synonymous to faeces. Worse still was a "Bryner", when the opponents score 100 counts before one was able to score. Dominoes were a lot of fun especially with the hard talk that accompanied the playing. We shifted the dominoes from Willie Thompson Alley to the bottom of Upper Fiennes Avenue and adjoining to Central street, next to a landmark which was known by simply what it was,' The Big Stone'. The host for these sessions was Mackie "Sticks" Procope. Mackie lived with his aging grandmother whom we all called Ma. Ma's hearing was seriously challenged so the noise we youngsters made never really bothered her and she greeted and welcomed us to her home and we all loved and respected Ma as if she was our own grandmother. We played dominoes mainly for fun, but sometimes we played ten—a—pass dominoes for one penny every time one was passed. A penny was also given to the player who first scored 100 counts, which was amassed from points from passes as well as points earned from winning hands. We experimented with gambling casino style by playing games like twenty one (blackjack), thirty one (similar to blackjack but dealing three cards instead of two). We played Bragg a simplified version of poker playing with three cards instead of seven or five cards, counting for straights, flushes, pairs and three of a kind and my favourite game we called Pepper. "Bobby" Archibald was always a sour looser and always had an argument about who did something wrong that caused him to have lost a hand and he also made the most noise in celebration when he was winning. Our stakes were usually one penny (2 cents) with a maximum raise of five cents. The disease of gambling did not go any further than these fun times for me. Unfortunately for some others it became a chronic disease that had led them to very embarrassing situations.

On the Whitsuntide weekend of 1966 a number of us from Mc Knight decided to go to Anguilla on an excursion by an inter-island schooner named Lady Mac. The trip was organized by Vernon Fleming, an Anguillan who operated a brokerage, shipping and associated services company. We were invited to go to Anguilla by another Anguillan who worked in St. Kitts and lived in Mc Knight in a house just behind our home on Shaw Avenue. We had developed a very good friendship. My friend's name was Angelo Thomas.

The round trip fare to Anguilla for the excursion on the Lady Mac was about twenty dollars. I got the fare from my father and was able to help myself with pocket money from the draw of our shop.

We sailed out of Pump Bay Harbour, Sandy Point on the Saturday evening. We left Basseterre by way of one of Fleming's flat bed trucks with many other persons. The Larro-Feeds Steel Band as well as a team of netballers from the Girl's High School was amongst us. I can also remember a number of gentlemen who were my senior being on the trip as well. Euclid Hanley and Rudolph Ottley are two that immediately come to my mind.

The pans for the Larro-Feeds Steel Band were loaded onto the Lady Mac along with other cargo of provisions and other staples, finally, the passengers all went on board.

It was a pleasant sail out of the harbour at Pump Bay at about midnight. We sat on the deck of the Lady Mac for about an hour. Then the boat started to rock. Somebody shouted that we were approaching Statia Channel—the body of water that lies between St. Kitts and the Dutch Territorial island of St. Eustatius. The bounce and sway of the Lady Mac started to become more and more pronounced. Then suddenly there was a huge wave that came crashing over the deck of our vessel. A number of us scattered from the above deck down into the hatch of the Lady Mac. The Lady Mac had huge junks of scrap metal in its hull which was used as ballasts. The metal in the hull were covered only by a canvas tarpaulin. It was uncomfortable but many of us endured that discomfort rather than to stay on deck and endure the battering from the waves that continued to break over the deck of the Lady Mac.

Many persons vomited. I can remember at the dawn of light somewhere between St. Martin and Anguilla one of the sailors opened the door of the hatch, looked in only to find a pot that they usually cooked in, filled with vomit to his amazement and disbelief. I guess a large portion of the vomit was contributed by the Girl's High School Netball Team. My guess is that I slept for most of the time we were in the hatch.

By daybreak we were sailing in much calmer water nearing the harbour on Anguilla. I was back on the deck then, looking at the several cays as we sailed past them as we continued our journey to our destination. We landed at Island Harbour. My most embarrassing moment came when all eyes were on me, when I vomited over the side of the vessel in the calmest of water; the only time that I vomited on the journey. The journey to Anguilla was a really rough one and many of us dreaded the return trip.

We left Island Harbour by way of car, Angelo had arranged for us to be picked-up by car, and we were driven to the Valley—capital town of Anguilla. We arrived at Angelo's family home where we were warmly welcomed by Angelo's mom, Mrs. Thomas, other family members and relatives.

We had breakfast. Soon thereafter we were on a foot-tour of the Valley. By midday we went to Crocus Bay and had a beautiful swim in the most tranquil water that was also crystal clear. We returned to Angelo's house for a sumptuous lunch of Anguillan rice and peas and stewed goat meat. We hung out near Angelo's home for some time playing dominoes

The evening we went to the cinema. The lighting and projectors were powered by a local generator as there was no central generating facility on the island at this time and only a few of the more affluent families and businesses had private electrical generators. I cannot remember what the movie was, but at the end of it we returned to Angelo's home and had a good night's rest.

The Monday morning, Whit Monday, we went to Borrower's Park to watch the Girl's High School Netball Teams play against Anguillan teams. We later went to an open area near the airport where there was an open air fete with lots of food and drink and plenty of dominoes. It was a big Anguillan social event, maybe it was a church bazaar. We met almost everyone who was on the boat at this function. I can remember a number of the men who could have afforded it financially, pool their resources together and chartered an aircraft to take them back to St. Kitts on the Whit Monday afternoon because of the discomfort of the outward journey. My dear friend Euclid was amongst those who flew back to St. Kitts.

By afternoon it was time for the matinee dance at the community centre. Larro-Feeds Steel Band provided the music. My best recollection of the scheduled time for the dance was from 2 o'clock in the afternoon to seven o'clock in the evening. There were a number of young and older persons at the dance. The Anguillan girls were quite friendly and we found no difficulty in finding partners to dance. I guess the Anguillan guys were focusing on the Girl's High School netballers. I made friends with a young lady and we corresponded with each other as pen-pals for about a year, our pen-pal relationship came to an end at about the time of the rebellion. We were in Anguilla some nine months or so before the rebellion broke out and I did not recognize any signs of hostility towards us as Kittitians.

By the time the evening shadows had covered the area, the gas lamps were turned on to provide lighting for the final stages of the dance and the packing up. After collecting our bags at Angelo's home we headed for Island Harbour. On the beach at Island Harbour there was a kind of a sending off party in the form of a bon-fire where we had roasted fish and other Anguillan goodies. We sailed out of Island Harbour in a perfect calm with the Lady Mac inching ahead primarily on the power of its engine. There was hardly a breeze. We had a slow but comfortable sail back to Pump Bay, Sandy Point and did not reach St. Kitts until about nine o'clock in the morning of the Tuesday. We journeyed to Basseterre just as the way we went down to Sandy Point two evenings earlier.

We the young men of Mc Knight rallied like a team, a brotherhood, and developed friendships that have had lasting currency.

During our adolescent years we read quite a lot of illustrated comic books. We exchanged comics amongst us as well as other youngsters from outside Mc Knight, as we acquired the comic books. We found and read some of the most sensuous bits of literature that we got our hands on. We read the "Kama Sutra of Love", "Fanny Hill" and many others. These were our early education in sexology. They stimulated our interest in women and sex.

I had fantasies about the woman whom I wanted in my life. In the nineteen sixties families guarded their daughters with tight security. The girls did not have the freedom to be up and about as they wished as is now seen in modern society. Teenage pregnancy was a rarity as compared to today, as the chance for a boy and girl to have sexual intercourse was remote. The girl that invaded my dreams and fantasies was my next door neighbour, Theresa. I have had a lifetime of love and admiration for this lady, a sensuous passion that has been pure and platonic up to this day. She left school before me and went to work. Unfortunately she never made it to the Girls' High School, and so at age sixteen she had to leave the Basseterre Senior School and found employment in the city. She became friendly with Lloyd, an athlete and national footballer. By the time I was out of school, I knew that I never had a chance of displacing Lloyd. They had a son together, Sean, I wished he was mine.

CHAPTER 9

Grammar School

The jamming as associated with the Christmas festivities was over. The masquerades had all washed and packed away their costumes. The ham and sorrel were all consumed in the manner that had become familiar to us. The first Monday of the New Year had come, the day when we would start our new journey through high school. I got up and did my usual chores of cleaning the yard, feeding the chickens and going to the bakery to get the bread for the shop. My Aunt Eunice made sure that I had a good breakfast. I showered and then got dressed for the St. Kitts Nevis Grammar School. The uniform for the SKNGS was short khaki pants, beige shirt, a tie with three horizontal bars alternating in red, blue and gold throughout its length, brown socks and brown shoes. A cap was optional but I never got one. Everything was brand new. I left our home at Shaw Avenue and went to the home of a fellow Mc Knighter, Ezerette Laws, who had also gained entrance to the Grammar School. I sat in the living room of their house while his grandmother did the final adjustments to his tie and made sure that everything was properly and smartly in place. Miss Josephine, as we all called her, came out of their front door a step behind us and watched us as we went through the alleyway and turned northwards on Fiennes Avenue, to start our trek to our new school. We got to the school and met a number of the debutants, some I knew while others were complete strangers. Many of the boys from Mrs. Warner's 1A from Basseterre Senior made the trip over and across the field. These included Patrick Knight, Lawson Estridge, Earnest Hendricks, Vincent Liburd and Raphael Payne. Payne and Liburd had topped the lists in the entrance exams and in addition to obtaining scholarships they were placed in second form.

The first strange thing I noticed at the Grammar School was that at roll call the surnames were called first, I thus became Williams, Clement

D. O. and not the Clement Williams that I had grown accustomed to all those years before. I was placed in 1B with twenty seven other young men. My desk was in the second row and to the extreme end to the right when facing the blackboard. The class was arrayed in a four by seven matrix. Within the first few weeks the eight of us on the right side of the class became a banded bunched; Edgar Galloway, Calvin Buchanan, Patrick Knight, Von Rebop Southwell, Earnest Hendricks, Vincent James and Dennis Berridge and me. We styled ourselves as the Republic.

The curriculum at the grammar school was much more extensive than what we had been exposed to at the Basseterre Senior School. French, metal work, woodwork and technical drawing were added to the core subjects. It took me a while to understand what was required at the grammar school with respect to study habits and home work assignments. We were provided with all the text books needed for the various subjects and two customized exercise books for each subject. Previously I did very little reading of any literature other than the comic books of the classics like "A Thousand Leagues Under the Sea" and the westerns of Billy the Kid, Wyatt Earp and Roy Rogers published by Dell Comics. I found it difficult to read and study several pages from the solid texts of "King Arthur" for Literature and the text of English History about the Normans and Plantagenets. My world of reading was mainly illustrated.

After six weeks in the first term, the first mark sheet came out. The guns who surfaced immediately were Alonzo 'Sausage' Jones, Joseph Edwards and Clement 'Tex' Edwards. Two guys from the Republic were in the cellar positions. The headmaster came to the class with the mark sheet, swinging a tamarind rod in his hand; that was terrifying. Mr. Riberio complimented the guys who did well at first and then went to the bottom of the ranking and with a different tone he reprimanded and cautioned the guys in the lower quadrant. I ranked number twenty on the first mark sheet. I felt relaxed as he was heading towards the door. Then he paused, turned back to the class and said that there were a few others whose performances were below the expected average. He asked who Williams, C. was. I stood up and he called about three other names. We were cautioned with a few threatening waves of the tamarind rod in the air, threatening that next time he would put it to use. That was good enough for me. By the second mark sheet I was wedging myself between the guns. I had subjects that I scored heavily on, the technical subjects, arithmetic, geometry, algebra and general science. These helped me to post an average that sky-rocketed me from the fringes of the lower quadrant to the upper echelons of the class. My overall position for the first term was eight from the top.

When the report for the first term came, my Aunt Eunice sat me down on a chair as she read through the report and then handed it back to me. She told me to read everything for her and she took up a four inch paint brush and held it by the bristles and pointed to the letter head which read 'St. Kitts Nevis Grammars School'. A dialogue ensured that went something like this:

"St. Kitts Nevis Grammar school" I said, as she pointed to another cell on the report sheet.

"Number of times late: twenty eight" was my response, I received a lash on the knuckle of my right hand. She pointed to another cell.

"Position in form: eighth" was my reply, I received another lash on my knuckles followed by her question.

"What happened to first, second and third?" Another lash was given to me as she pointed to another cell.

"English: forty four" I said, another lash.

"That is the language you are supposed to be talking every day." That was her response as she pointed to another cell.

"English Literature: thirty five." That was my reply. For that I received two lashes on the same right hand as the Literature mark was the lowest on the sheet. Then, the pointing continued.

"History: forty" I said in a tearful voice, more lashes in the same area.

"Latin: forty four" I paused and waited for the lash that was sure to come.

"French: thirty eight" another lash as the tears began to flow freely.

"Geography: seventy seven" I paused for a moment, and then she pointed again to another cell.

"Arithmetic: eighty seven" I said with some pride and arrogance, I received a tap on my shoulder with the same paint brush handle; it was a tap of commendation.

"Algebra: seventy six" I said with some confidence, my Aunt changed her style of interrogation and instead of going through the areas of my strength she jumped to the cell further down on the page.

"Form teacher's remarks: He has shown considerable improvement toward the end of term, but has too many weak areas, where he has to make every effort to improve" I read that with some doubt, not knowing what to anticipate. That was the icing on the cake and the lashes came to many parts of the body, everywhere except for my head and groin.

It was the Easter weekend and I was given a reward of one dollar to go to the movies at the Apollo cinema to see the movie "The Crucifixion" for doing well in the mathematical, science and technical subjects. That was a case of reward and punishment coming almost simultaneously.

The other two terms in first form went well for me; I was always in the top four for every mark sheet but never came first in class, it was Al Jones, Joe and Tex Edwards oscillating amongst the first position. I lost marks for poor grammar and spelling, even in my favourite subjects.

It was sometime in first form that I got the nickname Bouncin'. We had an Anguillan lady, Verna Richardson, who taught us English in the last term in first form and she affectionately called me Willy. There was a notorious character about Basseterre who was called "Bouncing Willy", so it was easy for the boys in The Republic to extend the name of "Bouncing Willy" to me. At the time they all had nicknames so it was only fitting that in time they had to find one for me. I guess the name somehow matched my physical size and stayed with me from then. As like so many of us Kittitians we are better known by our nicknames than our baptised name. I guess I accepted the name eventually. It became shortened to "Bouncin'" over a period of time.

The year in second form was the most challenging as we had only two terms to complete the curriculum instead of the accustomed three. This was the period of transition when the school year changed from January to December to September to August. This also brought the change from the Cambridge School Certificates to the General Certificate of Education (GCE) where the emphasis was on individual subjects. To get the Cambridge School Certificate one had to do well in subjects that were in some kind of a grouping. A typical grouping demanded that an acceptable mark had to be scored in English Language, English Literature, mathematics, a science subject and a modern language. I was lucky that that change came at a time when I was able to capitalize on it.

In second form, 2B, we met a number of repeaters and two or three boys who were transferred from Convent School. I managed to sustain a position in the top ten of the class, I did not do as well as I did in 1B but I was determined that I would capitalize on the short year. In second form, it was said that three of us were identical in appearance: Roland Benjamin, Von Re bop Southwell and I. Mr. Riberio always confused us; he would call me Southwell or Benjamin on many occasions. One day we went to the Wood Work shop, Benjamin turned on the drill press and told Stanley Charles to stall the rotating chuck with his hand. Playing with machinery was prohibited in the shop. The teacher, Mr. Arnold Warner, arrived just in time to see Charles holding on to the lever of the drill press. He was caught red-handed. Mr. Warner enquired from Stanley who gave him permission to turn on the drill press. His reply was that it was I who had turned on the machinery. Mr. Warner sent both Stanley and me to the headmaster's office. I protested and stated that it was not I who had turned on the machine. Mr. Riberio passed judgment and summarily sentenced both of us to three strokes with the tamarind rod. I protested further and pleaded my innocence, which was the truth. The machine was turned on by Roland Benjamin and Charles, the most diminutive in the class, insisted that it was I who had turned the machine on and told him to stall it with his hand. My only defence was that he, the headmaster himself, on many occasions confused Benjamin and me for each other. I guess he recalled at least one such occasion. He sent Charles to call Benjamin. When Benjamin arrived at the office he categorically denied that it was he who had turned on the drill press and gave Charles the challenge to stall it. He admitted that he was in the shop before Mr. Warner had arrived. The headmaster then enquired if we were sure that we were not brothers, with a sense of humour. The headmaster resolved the situation by giving all three of us one hundred and fifty lines each. The line pertained to safety in the shops, and it was a long line. That saved me from the ordeal of the tamarind rod for the second time. The only previous occasion on which I was flogged was in 1B, for coming to school late three times in one week. Throughout my early years at grammar school I was the king of late detention. One of the tasks for late detention was to do work on the paving slab for the combination basketball and tennis court north of the auditorium. The school borrowed a concrete mixer and every afternoon we cast a section of the court as was laid out. I can remember the headmaster directing me to take a wheel barrow of concrete from a sixth former who was struggling with it; I was physically bigger and stronger than the sixth former.

The only other occasion that I got strokes in Grammar School was for going to Latin class without a text book for Latin translations. I had lent mine to a fifth former who never brought it back for me. It was in one of Mr. Riberio's bad weeks when explanations were accepted only after punishment. I got two lashes with the tamarind rod. When I gave my excuse for not having the Latin translation book, I was sent to get the fifth former. He admitted that he had the book but it was at home. He was sent home immediately to collect the book after a stern reprimand from the headmaster. I got the book back.

The final exams were taken and I did well enough to go on to third form; I was placed in 3T (technical) where we did the technical options whereas those in 3A took the language options. 3T was easier for me as I got the burdens of French and Latin lifted from my shoulders. I chose technical drawing and metal work as my alternatives. In 3T we were introduced to chemistry, physics and biology as single subjects, a big advantage for me. I began featuring in the top five of the class. I can remember once we had a history chapter to study for a test, it dealt with the reorganizing of England after the Industrial Revolution. It dealt with the application of James Watts' steam engine to industry, and the development of the Mc Adams method of road paving, down to the reorganization of the British Police Force. I took special interest in that chapter and studied it thoroughly; I did a lot of self-testing and was ready for whatever Mr. J B C Haynes the History Master had to throw at us. Mr. Haynes came to the class only to announce that he had to help the Headmaster with something urgently and he would not be giving the test that day and we should go ahead and read the next chapter under the supervision of the monitor. We never came back to that chapter. At the end of the third form year, when the final examinations were completed I tore my junior school tie of red, gold and blue to shreds with a sense of confidence and arrogance. I was certain that I no longer had use for it.

Fourth form was next, in 4B. We wore long trousers and a tie with only two colours: red and blue in horizontal bars throughout the length of it. My two best subjects turned out to be Geography and Chemistry. These were the two subjects that had a lot of punishment for poor marks on tests and homework assignments. Mr. David Wright, an English V S O (Voluntary Service Overseas) taught us Geography. There were long hours of detention. Mr. Frank Mills taught us Chemistry and likewise the pain of writing every definition one got wrong in a test ten times and every chemical equation fifteen times forced me to prepare and study these subjects well. I proved to myself that I was better than those who were detained. For the first time in my history in school I came first in class on mark sheets as well as first overall in the second term. Surprisingly the worst performance on average for the class was in the subjects that I topped the class in. We had the indefatigable J W Sutton for our literature teacher, the same man who was my headmaster at Basseterre Boys. He had a different style of marking from all other teachers, he demanded that all answers had to be given in full sentences and deducted a quarter mark for every spelling or grammatical mistake. Somehow I managed to survive the deductions and was given literature as one of my subjects in fifth form.

In fifth form we had a curriculum that provided for a maximum of seven subjects; chemistry and geography were placed in the same group as an either or for us to choose one. This made me mad. I had to choose between the two subjects that I had worked so hard for. I can remember when we went to 5B; Mr. Wright came to me in a rage, questioning me how it was that I did not choose Geography when I got the best marks in the subject in the fourth form exams. He recalled that I got eighty two percent. I laughed and said to him I got ninety one percent in chemistry. That was the end of our debate about my choice of chemistry over geography. In those days of Grammar School education, the curriculum was rigid and there was no leeway for me to do both. In modern times I would have dropped History and have Mr. Wright set-up individualized instructions at times of mutual convenience to both of us. I was not afforded that choice which demonstrated the great advantage that is now enjoyed by the comprehensive education system of today. When the geography examination was done in the May /June sitting Mr. Wright brought the paper to show me. I was certain that from my work in fourth form and my general knowledge that I would have had geography added to my list of subjects passed.

English language continued to be a disaster for me. I knew my marks for every essay that I submitted even before the topic was given. It was eight on twenty, followed by the standard comment "great ideas but too many spelling and grammatical errors". The year in fifth form went by, and by the time we got to registration for Cambridge GCE O'levels I had convinced the Headmaster that it was a waste of time for me to do history. I was registered for English Language, English Literature, mathematics, physics, biology and chemistry. The cost for registering for six subjects at that time was twenty-two dollars and sixty cents. The results returned were no surprise to me; they were passes in mathematics, physics and biology, a distinction in chemistry and outright failures in the other two.

In September 1966, I was allowed to go on to sixth form to take chemistry, mathematics and physics on condition that I attended extra classes in English that were organized by the school. These classes were tutored by a Mr. Travis Phillips. I failed English for a second time in June 1967 at the same time topping the lower sixth class results in additional mathematics. The next year, in 6A, I passed one A'level (Chemistry) and O' level English Language. I officially left school on June 10, 1968 having completed my A'level exams.

The full implementation of the comprehensive secondary education on St. Kitts was done during my last year in school. The St. Kitts Nevis Grammar School, the Girls High School and the Basseterre Senior School were merged to become the Basseterre High School and The Basseterre Junior High School under two separate and distinct administrations. The Basseterre Junior High provided for the first and second forms plus a remedial program for those who were deemed not capable enough to go on to the third form of the Basseterre High for final examinations at GCE O'level at the end of fifth form. The sixth form then was still at the Basseterre High. That year a school year-book was produced which featured the individual students that graduated from the O'level and the A'level classes of 1968 as well as photos of staff and of extra-curricular activities of the school.

The senior boys, fourth form and above, were permitted to join the Debating Society and the Co-Ed Club. We dressed in the official formal wear of the school that was the school uniform with a navy blue blazer that had the school crest with the school's motto "Principia Non Homines" etched on it. The meetings of the Debating Society and Co-Ed club were alternated on Friday nights. At the Debating Society there were only boys from the Grammar School in attendance whereas at the Co-Ed club, girls from the Girls High School came over to join us. The Co-Ed club was a social gathering where we played games, had dance classes, fetes and other healthy activities for teenagers. For me this was a period of my life when I was really proud to be going to the Grammar School, strutting across the city of Basseterre early evenings on a Friday wearing a blazer was seen as a mark of achievement by all whom one passed on the way to the school's auditorium.

While in sixth form, Mr. Eustace Esdaille was our teacher of General Paper, a subject that examined world affairs, societal concerns and attitudes. He also taught English Literature at O and A levels. He was the master responsible for the school's Drama Society. Every Speech Day an extract from one of the plays on the literature curriculum was selected and produced. Some years the full play was produced and staged as a fund-raiser for the school. During November and December 1966 the play chosen was Shakespeare's "Julius Caesar". The hotshots of the drama society were given the big parts, Vincent Bergan was Caesar, Juni Liburd was Mark Anthony and Henry "Stogumber" Browne was Cassius. I was drafted as a Roman soldier who had only three lines to say in the entire play. Even though it was that simple, I dreaded what would be the outcome. In those days when you were drafted to do anything for the school, objecting would be a waste of time and effort. I did my part and assisted with the stage management.

St. Kitts and Nevis was granted Internal Self Government with full responsibility for internal affairs with Britain retaining responsibilities for Foreign Affairs and Defence, in 1967. Our new political status was labelled as an Associated State to Britain. As part of the celebrations for the attainment of Statehood there was a play-writing competition. The best plays were chosen for production. Eustace Esdaille was appointed as the producer. Three short plays were on the bill. I was drafted as the postman in the play "Not Pen-Pals but one". This play was directed by Cromwell Ira Bowry. When I first read the script I thought the part of the postman was a minor part so I was comfortable with it. I must have done that part so well that at the curtain call I, like the two lead characters Abdo (played by Al Jones) and his Anguillan pen-pal (played by Maureen Adams) got standing ovations. It was like a spiritual baptism from the outpouring of the love and appreciation that came to me from the audience. There and then I thought I found my niche in society. My biggest fan was the Deputy Principal of the School, Mrs Eileen Thompson. I can remember Mrs. Thompson remarking to me that she never realized that I had so much energy, as she always thought of me as the big lazy boy who lumbered across the road from campus to campus.

In later years as I grew in producing and directing drama she was present at every production that I staged during her lifetime.

We travelled to Nevis to do the Statehood production. Again, we got the same response from the audience. It was a fantastic experience.

At the end of our sixth form years, a group of us from the lower and upper sixth forms and some young teachers decided that we would raise some funds and travel to Trinidad at the end of the school year by way of one of the two federal ships. They were the Palm and the Maple. We had several fund raising activities. The biggest was a concert and dance where we had erected on the basketball court an open air stage. We featured the varied talents in song and dance of many students as well as outstanding guest artistes from outside the school. The band we engaged for the show was a group from within the school. We featured models in a fashion show where we got a number of boutiques in the city and top seamstresses to offer their pieces for display. From that they got some advertisement and recognition. The final performance on the stage show was a one act play called "Mamaguy" written by Trinidadian Freddie Kissoon. The story of the original script demanded that one of the main characters had to dress as and play the part of a woman, so as to fool the rich Uncle who had just arrived from the United States, into believing that he was the wife of his buddy. None of the big actors amongst us wanted to play the part of the cross-dresser. The play was humorous and we were certain that it would be a big hit. I took the liberty to rewrite Freddie Kissoon's story. I transformed the major conflict in the play from a lie about wife and child to support in hard times to the main character not being able to account for a house that he should have bought for his Uncle who had sent the money for him to purchase it. I had to cast myself as Lennox in the play and played against the stage gun in school. At that time Henry 'Stogumber' Browne played the lead character, Rupert. The response to the play was as if it was a second baptism. Nothing less spiritual than the one I had experienced when I did the Statehood plays. That was the beginning of the now famous "Bouncin—Stogumber" stage duo. The dance followed, and music was supplied by the Silver Rhythm Combo. It was a grand occasion and we secured some good profits.

Another fund raiser was the occasion when we hosted a formal invitation dance. Couples, young and old were invited. We had settings of chairs and tables on the basketball court with decorations and coloured lighting to create a classy ambience. Dancing was in the auditorium, on a waxed floor; again with music from the Silver Rhythm Combo. We ran a bar where we sold all types of liquors, beer, malts and soft drinks. The ladies provided a stall where they served hot dogs, hamburgers and other snacks. We had over two hundred couples attending, at five dollars a couple plus donations, we made in excess of one thousand dollars. The older folks really enjoyed themselves as this dance was different from the common form of dances which were described as "wash you foot and come".

We subsidised our trip with less than thirty dollars per person for the tour on the boat and our food and accommodation at the St. Augustine Campus of the University of the West Indies for the five days we spent in Trinidad. The party of us, who took the trip, joined the Federal Maple on its southbound trip, sometime in late July. We left Basseterre late in the evening. The first stop of our cruise was at Plymouth, Montserrat. The water was choppy and that made it difficult for tendering, so tendering was limited. Not many of us got to go ashore on Montserrat as priority was given to the Montserratians who were leaving or joining the ship.

The second day brought us to Antigua. The weather was much better and the long tender ride to the pier from the ship was simply interesting. We walked all over St. Johns, buying food from restaurants, and visiting some persons whom members of the group had had contact with.

We arrived in Dominica on the third day. This was the point where the two sister ships crossed, one northbound the other southbound. After tendering to shore, we walked the streets of Roseau, exploring the shops and market places, buying fruits and food for that day.

On the fourth day we docked at Castries harbour, St. Lucia. This harbour allowed easy access to and from the ship as we went about exploring Castries.

Day five was spent in Barbados. We docked at Bridgetown deepwater port. We walked to Pelican Village and then to the city. We explored Bridgetown during the early part of that day. Later a group of us got a minivan to take us to the Cave Hill Campus of the University of the West Indies. One of our comrades, Leroy Crosse, had gained entrance to Cave Hill and he wanted to see the place. We got to Cave Hill, identified who we were and a young man from the administration gave us a tour of the facilities. We had lunch in the cafeteria and looked through the library and bookstore for some time before we walked down the long hill back to the main road and caught a Barbados Transport Board bus which took us back to the city. We hung out for a while, as well as traversed the city back and forth; making acquaintance with folks we met, until it was time to get back to the ship.

Day six was St. Vincent. We docked at the newly built harbour in Kingstown. It was Saturday and this gave us an opportunity to mix with the ordinary folks on market day. The open market near the docks was exciting. We walked and explored the city as well as the nearby environs of Arnos Vale. By then we had developed a routine mode of operations, making sure that we got back to the ship before sailing time.

Sunday was the seventh day of our trip and it brought us to Grenada. We docked at St. Georges Harbour. In Grenada we were met by a group of Jaycees personnel. One of our group members was a member of the Jaycees, and Edwin Glasford had made some arrangement with the group to host us for the day. All arrangements were beautifully in place. We had a tour of a section of the island and made a call on the Governor of Grenada, Dame Hilda Bynoe at her official residence. After the tour, we were then taken to Grand Anse Bay for a beach picnic where we were provided with lunch. Grenada was fantastic.

The final stop southbound was Trinidad. We spent from Monday morning to Friday evening of that week going between Port of Spain and St. Augustine Campus of the University of the West Indies. We took the public transport buses from the terminal near the harbour to the UWI Campus. We were accommodated at Milner Hall. Each of us had our own room with common bathroom facilities. The cost at Milner Hall covered breakfast. We explored Trinidad. The buses were cheap. It was about fifteen cents for a ride from St. Augustine to Port of Spain. After breakfast each day we chose one of the major cities to explore. We went east to Arima, west to St. James, Diego Martin and Careenage and South to San Fernando, passing the massive oil refinery at Point a Pierre. Trinidad was a most enriching experience.

Some days we took the train that ran from Tunapuna to Port of Spain. The train rides were cheaper than the buses; it was eight cents from St. Augustine to Port of Spain. The train stop was just outside the main gate to the UWI campus. We met Frenrick, Stogumber's cousin who was a train driver. Stogumber had made telephone contact with some of his relatives that had migrated to Trinidad in the late 1920's, as part of the black gold rush, petroleum, when many of our people went there to seek employment. He met an uncle and an aunt who were native Nevisians. An arrangement was made for us to join the train on a morning when Frenrick was the train driver and we journeyed to Port of Spain by rail. We limed in Port of Spain until Frenrick had finished his shift at one o'clock. He met us at the bus terminal and took us by bus to his mother's house in Upper Bourne's Road in St. James. We met Stogumber's aunt and other members of the family. We were told about another aunt who was the mother of the Burroughs brothers. The Burroughs brothers were the famed Randolph Burroughs, who became Commissioner of Police in Trinidad and Tobago and the younger brother who was a Superintendent of the Fire Services at that time. They also were first generation descendants of Nevis. We actually met the younger brother who took Stogumber and me in his Austin Cambridge motor car on tour one evening right out west up to Careenage and Tetron Bay.

I spent my twentieth birthday in the company of a long standing pen-pal. Her name was Rosario James of #2 Cotton Hill, Long Circular Road, St. Clair, Port of Spain. I got there by taxi. I was introduced to her mother and older sister and we had lunch together. After lunch we walked to the nearby zoo and botanical gardens. That was a most pleasant experience which I enjoyed immensely. I left the James' early afternoon and headed back to St. Augustine by means of public transport.

On the Friday, most of us set off for San Fernando on the bus that stopped from village to village as we explored South Trinidad. It was fun seeing people of different races and colour intermingling in the day's activities around the bus stops and stands, selling and haggling over all kinds of wares, fruits and provisions. We explored the city of San Fernando and made sure that we visited on the famous Coffee Street. For our return journey we took the express bus back up to the north and were advised by the bus conductor that it would be better for us if we got off at the Curepe Junction and then take a bus up to St. Augustine. We got back to St. Augustine and packed our bags to make the journey back to the ship.

We checked in and got on board before six in the evening. We were on early, so that we could get bunks in the lower deck. Many of the travellers slept on the upper deck under a canvas covering. They slept on benches as well as on the deck itself on blankets and other makeshift beds.

After I had secured my bunk, I decided that I would venture to the James' home in St. Clair to say goodbye. Outside the port gate I flagged down a taxi and asked the driver to take me to the St. Clair Police Station. In Trinidad there are route taxis that run specific routes, the taxi I got was a St. James taxi. I guess the driver responded to police station and not the specifics of St. Clair. I was the lone passenger and we had a nice friendly conversation as we drove along the Western Main Road. I was dropped at the St. James Police Station only to recognize that I was in the wrong place. I went to the guard desk inside the police station and spoke to an officer who was in attendance and explained my predicament. His advice to me was that I could get to the St. Clair Police Station by walking along the road outside the front of the station through Federation Park and continuing until I got to St. Clair Police Station. By then it began to get dark. I walked the journey, and noted the signs of the various avenues named after the various islands that were part of the defunct West Indies Federation. I got to the St. Clair Police Station; my landmark for the James' residence that was exactly opposite on the other side of the road. I was a bit scared. I worried about getting back to the boat on time. I reached my destination and called at the residence of my long standing pen-pal and her family. I mounted the steps and was greeted by her big sister. I was invited in and we were joined by Mom and my pen-pal. I outlined my ordeal of the hour before. My goodbye stay was shortened. Mom gave me an outline on the transportation system in Trinidad and gave instructions how to get to St. Clair from downtown Port of Spain by the various means of public transportation. By this time my pen-pal had prepared a sandwich for me with a glass of orange juice. I had the snack and shortly thereafter Mom ordered an executive taxi from a nearby hotel to take me back to the port. Mrs. James paid for the taxi which delivered me back to the port with ample time to catch the Maple. We sailed out of Port of Spain harbour at about eleven o' clock that night.

The Northward bound journey was a mere repetition of the southbound journey only in a reverse order.

In Grenada, while on our ups and down through St. Georges, I recognized a person whom I knew very well. It was the Right Honourable Sir Robert Llewellyn Bradshaw, then Premier of St. Kitts and Nevis, about to enter the Barclay's Bank. I greeted him and he instantly recognized me. In his usual stern style, he asked what I was doing there. I pointed out the other members of the group who were with me at that time and explained our mission. He wished us well and safe journeys in our travels back to St. Kitts. He continued his way and we ours.

In St. Vincent we followed the same routine as the earlier stop. In addition, some members of our group went to church in the early morning of Sunday.

Barbados was the exception. Travelling north with us was a choir group from one of the established churches in Barbados. In a few days we became very friendly with some members of the Barbados group. Fortunately, the Maple spent two days in Barbados on the northward journey. On the second day we were invited to the home of a Mr. Bellamy, a mechanic who had his own garage and repair shop in Green Hill, St. Michaels. We took the Rockley bus as prescribed by our new friend and arrived safely at his home. We were introduced to his wife and family and he showed us around the garage. We later had a sumptuous lunch of fried chicken with options of rice and red beans, potatoes and a green salad. We had lots of coconut water spiked with a little Mount Gay Rum for those of us who wanted to experiment. We had a good time with Baje, as we called him, and his family.

The extra day in Barbados was remedied by doing Montserrat and Antigua in one day. We got into Montserrat early and set sail about one in the afternoon. We were in St. Johns by four o'clock, three hours later.

We got back to the Basseterre Roadstead on the Saturday morning with sea legs after almost three weeks of touring the Eastern Caribbean States and Trinidad. This trip was a fitting end to my journey of almost seven years as a student of the St. Kitts Nevis Grammar School and Basseterre High School.

CHAPTER 10

In The Labour Movement

I went to vote for the first time when I was eight years old; I was taken by my mother to the Basseterre Magistrates Courts building on Lozac Road where she went to vote in a referendum which was about St. Kitts, Nevis and Anguilla being part of the West Indies Federation. She voted YES! She acclaimed that her vote was to secure my future in what was anticipated to be the saviour of all the peoples of the West Indies; living together in harmony under one flag and as one country. The Labour Movement had campaigned for a 'yes' vote in the referendum.

The West Indies Federation included ten states that were all originally British colonies in the English speaking Caribbean. They were from north to south: Jamaica, St. Kitts—Nevis—Anguilla, Montserrat, Antigua and Barbuda, Dominica, St. Lucia, Barbados, St. Vincent and the Grenadines, Grenada and Trinidad and Tobago. The total land mass was about eight thousand square miles with a population of about four million people of great ethnic diversity which included the African (Blacks), Indians (Hindus and Moslems), Chinese, Arabs (Lebanese and Syrians), white Europeans (Portuguese, French, Spanish, Irish and English) the indigenous Amerindian people; as well a great proportion of mixed race people.

The West Indies Federation was short lived. It lasted from January 3, 1958 to May 31, 1962. The flag had a background of royal blue representing the Caribbean Sea, four waves running across the flag in white representing the waves of the sea and a golden orange circle in the centre representing the sun. It was described as the flag of sun and sea. The coat of Arms had two brown pelican on guard with a motto "To dwell together in unity". I cannot remember us singing a Federation Anthem but we sang a song that was composed and sung by a popular local calypsonian called King Leader, the lyrics were:-

Everywhere West Indians start to say

A nation is born today

Kittitians are proud to belong to the nation

Educate, cooperate it's a great federation

Blessed be the flag of sun and sea

As we dwell together in unity

Be a diamond amongst rubies

The mother colony of the West Indies.

The West Indies Federation was to remain part of the Commonwealth of Nations as a Constitutional Monarchy with Queen Elizabeth II remaining as Head of State and the Governor General was Lord Hailes, an English Baron, who represented her Majesty. Federal Elections of March 25, 1958 saw the Federal Labour Party being elected to form the first and only government of the Federation. The Federal House had 45 elected members and the results showed that the Federal Labour Party (FLP) won 26 seats and the Democratic Labour Party (DLP) 19 seats. Most of the FLP seats came from the smaller islands whereas the DLP had the majority of seats from Jamaica and Trinidad and Tobago. The only small island seat that was won by the DLP was that of St. Vincent and the Genadines. The Prime Minister of the Federation was The Honourable Grantley H. Adams of Barbados, and our own The Honourable Robert L. Bradshaw became the Senior Minister and Minister of Finance in the Cabinet of ten ministers. The federal capital was earmarked for Chaguaramas, Trinidad. In addition to our elected representative, there were two Senators from St. Kitts and Nevis, the Honourables William Seaton and James W. Liburd.

None of the well known, big named politicians of Jamaica and Trinidad took part in the Federal Elections. Even though Norman Manley and Alexander Bustamante were instrumental in organizing the two opposing factions, The Federal Labour Party and The Democratic Labour Party respectively, none of these two men contested for a seat in the Federal Parliament. They both went through the Caribbean helping the candidates from their respective parties with their campaigns. Eric Williams, who had not long gained political power as the Chief Minister of Trinidad and Tobago, did not take part in the Federal elections either.

The Bustamante faction, The Democratic Labour Party, having failed to gain power in the Federal elections started to agitate against the concept of the West Indian Federation in Jamaica. His vociferous campaigns forced a referendum in Jamaica which resulted in Jamaica leaving the Federation. This was the catalyst that brought about the total dismantling of the Federation. After Jamaica pulled out, that gave rise to a famous quotation that has been attributed to Dr. Eric Williams:—"One from ten leaves nought (zero)". After the demise of the Federation of 1958-62, Jamaica gained separate independence from Britain on August 6, 1962 and Trinidad and Tobago just days later on August 31, 1962. There were talks about a Federation of The Little Eight but no real progress was made as Barbados opted for Independence in 1966. The other seven territories were granted a political status that was termed as Associated Statehood, with each state having its own constitution and responsibility for its Internal Affairs with Britain being responsible for External Affairs and Defence. Each state Government was led by a Premier, The Hon. R. L. Bradshaw became the first Premier of St. Kitts and Nevis on February 27, 1967.

The demise of the West Indian Federation is well summarised in a calypso by the Mighty Sparrow.

The concept of Federation had taken hold on the people of the region, and rightfully so. A lot of pride was generated in us as a people. We were all West Indians and proud about it. Before the Federation we had already had the West Indies Cricket Team, with Sir Garfield Sobers having broken the world record for the highest individual score of 365 not out, which was made on the eve of the West Indies Federation coming together. His world record was sustained for over thirty six years before it was broken by another West Indian—Brian Lara in 1995. We had already had the University College of the West Indies (UCWI) that became an independent institution in 1962 as the University of the West Indies (UWI). There was a common currency in nine of the Federal States, the exception being Jamaica that was still using the British pounds sterling. The British West Indian dollar was recognized everywhere in Jamaica and everyone knew its equivalence or parity with the pound sterling. The two boats that were given to the Federal Government by Canada as an independence gift, MV Federal Palm and MV Federal Maple, served as integrating threads to help bind the people into an oneness. They facilitated trade and travel within the Federation and were operated by the West Indies Shipping Services. There were also the West Indies Supreme Courts, the West Indies Meteorological Services and the West Indian Regiment. These were all essential services that were under the direct responsibility of the Federal Government. The Federal Government had very little financial strength as they could not levy any form of direct income taxes on the people of the Federation but depended heavily on grants from Britain and contributions from the different territories with Jamaica and Trinidad and Tobago providing about 80% of the federal budget. The local state budget of Trinidad and Tobago and that of Jamaica were each separately bigger than the federal budget. I was indoctrinated to be a Federalist.

My father was one of the early pioneers in the Labour Movement and was always actively involved with the activities of the Trades and Labour Union and the Workers League—now the Labour Party. I guess there might have been some type of political infusion that spilled over to my mother. She was always vocal about political and social issues. I was born to parents who were stalwarts of the Labour Movement and thus have inherited a strong legacy within the Labour Movement of St. Kitts and Nevis. I can remember being taken by my mother on Labour Day to the marches of the union. The members of the union wore a red and white pin-on button with the inscription of UNION in blocked bold letters across the face of the button. I can remember my mother pinning one such button on my shirt as we walked from Newtown to join with the march. I was labelled UNION and eventually LABOUR all my life. I went to political meetings and rallies, holding on to my mother's frock tail from a very early age. The general election of 1956 saw the Workers League winning all the contested seats. The opposing side was the Democratic Party that was comprised mainly of planters and merchants. The Democrats had an aeroplane that flew over the city and bombarded the area with posters and flyers with their campaign material. The Workers League had men on foot, mounting posters on lampposts with flour and starch paste.

I can remember going to the meetings of the 1961 general elections campaign. While the Hon. R.L. Bradshaw was in the Federal House, he could not run for a seat in local Legislative Council at the same time. He was replaced by the Hon. Milton P. Allen for the Central Basseterre seat on the Workers League/Labour Party ticket. The slogan of the Central Basseterre campaign was "A Vote for Allen is a Vote for Bradshaw". M.P. Allen, like all the other Labour Party candidates won his seats in the Legislative Council. By this time the opposing party was the Peoples Progressive Movement (PPM) that was lead then by Lawyer Maurice Davis and which comprised mainly of blacks, mullato and Lebanese professionals and businessmen. The Hon. R. L. Bradshaw described the opposing candidates as 'errand boys' of the planters and merchants. I can remember the political leader of the Workers League/ Labour Party composing his campaign song and singing it. The lyrics were:—

When it's Christmas in November

We are not voting for you

When it comes to Maurice Davis

We are not voting for you

Again we say to Procope

We are not voting for you

And to Samuels and Astaphan

We are not voting for you.

My personal involvement in political affairs started with the introduction of Young Labour, which was the youth arm of the St. Kitts, Nevis Labour Party. The first Young Labour convention was held sometime in 1966 and the venue was at the Old Grammar School building (now the site of the Dr. William Connor Primary School) on a Sunday afternoon. There were hundreds of young people drawn from all areas of the island of St. Kitts as well as a delegation from Nevis. The main activities of that convention were to present a draft constitution for Young Labour and to elect an executive to see about the affairs of the youth movement. The names that were tossed about as the potential chairman of the national executive were those of Joseph Archibald, Fitzroy Bryant and Probyn Innis. Bryant eventually emerged as the Chairman.

One of the first tasks of the elected executive was to establish branches in various parts of the country. The three constituencies of Basseterre had one unified branch, whereas some constituencies had two branches depending on the geographical layout. For example even though West Farm, Boyd's, Trinity and Challengers were part of the West Basseterre Constituency they had their own branch. Young Labour helped to identify the leadership in the different areas of the country; they played pivotal roles in the election campaigns by mounting posters and billboards throughout the country and monitored the electoral lists. The leaders of the various branches were drawn together for special political education and awareness. We were housed in retreat camps for weekends with seminars, lecture presentations and field trips to various places of interest. Most of these retreat camps were held on long weekends where the Monday was a public holiday. We built makeshift housing in the yard of our then political leader, the Right Excellency Honourable Sir Robert L. Bradshaw while at the same time occupying a section of his house at Fortlands. We ate, drank and communicated politics for the entire period of our stay in those retreats. Young Labour provided the Labour Party with a line of potential candidates for succession.

My first article on political issues was published in the Labour Spokesman during the campaign of the 1966 elections. I wrote then under the name of PHYTON (fight—on). We were encouraged by the leadership of the party to write and publish in the Labour Spokesman. A weekly columnist was the Voice of Youth, which was written by a dear friend and comrade of mine. The Basseterre Young Labour was a very active group. We held meetings from five to seven on Friday evenings at Masses House, on Church Street, the headquarters of the Labour Movement. They involved a full spectrum of activities designed to keep the young people politically alert and with a strong social conscience. They involved debates, guest lecturers, dance class and visits to other branches.

I can remember one Sunday morning The Hon. Sam Terrance Condor and myself copying the lyrics of "Hark the Sound of Holy Voices" from a hymn book, because we wanted to be able to sing the full song in response to the lead of our political leader, at a meeting at Warner Park that night. By the time the 1966 General Elections were called I was heavy in the political campaign, stringing flags and buntings helping to decorate and erect stages where rallies were to be held throughout the island. The opponents then were the newly formed People's Action Movement (PAM), led by lawyer Dr. William V. "Billy" Herbert. The campaign song, penned by our political leader and sung to the melody of Jamaican bandleader Byron Lee's "Sunset Jump up", the modern version of the melody is called "St. Thomas" and the lyrics were:—

The Billy may skip and jump but pay him no mind

And Simmonds may walk and wine but leave him behind

Caines may grin

Powell may sing

Leave them far and vote for Labour.

On polling day I was actively, running messages on my bicycle, to and from polling stations to the Central Basseterre Campaign Headquarters upstairs Masses House. I felt left out as I had not attained the age of majority, which was twenty one years, which meant that I could not vote. The night of the counting of votes was really interesting. At that time the People's Action Movement headquarters was directly opposite to Masses House. PAM mounted loud speakers to broadcast the counts box by box. Crowds were mingling about Church Street and listening to counts as they were given by the Supervisor of Elections. By late in the night, the loudspeakers of PAM faded into silence and then the loudspeakers of the Labour Party at Masses House began blaring out the results, way down into the wee hours of the next morning. As the results grew more and more favourable for the Labour Party, the people came to fill Church Street for its entire length, wall to wall, until the people were addressed by their victorious candidates. The feting and merry making started there and then. I am pretty certain that the day after the polling was declared a Public Holiday. The following Sunday we went on an island wide motorcade celebrating labour's seven—nil victory over PAM.

In 1967 there was political turmoil in St. Kitts. The unitary State of St. Kitts Nevis and Anguilla was scheduled to gain Statehood on February 27. The Anguillans resisted statehood within the Unitary State; and decided to break away from St. Kitts and Nevis by unilaterally declaring themselves as an independent country. They discharged the central government representative, the Warden Mr. Vincent Byron, the contingent of the police force stationed on the Island, and some utility workers from the Electricity Department and Public Works who were there to do infrastructural work on the island. The people of Anguilla through their leadership waged an armed rebellion to effect these outcomes. It is recorded in many bits of literature, written by the people who were directly involved in the armed rebellion on Anguilla and the invasion of St. Kitts by armed Anguillans and mercenaries on the morning of June 10, 1967. The prime purpose of the invasion was to overthrow the Robert Bradshaw Government and install a government that would be more sympathetic to the Anguillan cause.

On the evening of June 9, 1967, a group of my friends from the Lower Sixth Form and I went to the sugar factory to look for sugar cane juice and generally observe the operations of the sugar factory. It was a customary thing for youngsters to go to the factory. We all went home with the intention to meet at the 12-6 dance at the Factory Social Centre. I slept the night through until I was awakened by the repeated volleys of gunshots and explosions. At that time it was only my father and my little sister and I living at Shaw Avenue. My father called my sister Yvette and I and he took us to sit in the stairwell at the back of our house where we were relatively safe, between concrete walls, from any of the bullets that were being discharged. We sat there until we could see the break of dawn coming through a partially opened window and the sound of the artillery had subsided by then. That was a horrifying experience, especially as we did not know what was going on. By full daylight people were wandering all about trying to find out what was going on, as well as wondering about what had taken place just hours before. The stories and the outcome of the invasion of June 10, 1967, and its repercussions are well documented by persons who were directly involved or those who were directly affected by the events of that day. The People's Action Movement has always been heavily implicated as being co-conspirators with the Anguillans and the sinister plots of June 10, 1967. A number of the executive officers of PAM and many of their supporters were detained and charged with various offences under the State of Emergency Regulations. The Bradshaw Government declared a State of Emergency soon after the armed attack of June 10, 1967. These matters were taken to the courts. Eventually the trials were discontinued by the government and all detainees were set free.

The year 1967 marked the beginning of the great political polarization within St. Kitts. Families were torn apart, best friends became enemies. Socialization within the society was based on political orientation, PAM or Labour, rather than the different elements of colour, race or wealth which were the measures by which our society had been previously stratified. Even in death, the political polarization was evident. The funeral home which looked after the interment was dependent on the political orientation of the family of the deceased. Political polarization has continued to be the greatest hindrance to the development of our beloved nation.

CHAPTER 11

Teaching as a Non-Graduate Assistant Teacher

The Monday morning immediately after our return to St. Kitts from our Eastern Caribbean Tour, I embarked on what turned out to become my lifelong career in education. All persons who had applied for jobs as teachers and were accepted by the Ministry of Education were invited to attend an induction course of training. In excess of fifty candidates, aspiring to become teachers, showed up at the premises of the old Cunningham Hospital on Burdon Street, Mc. Knight. The site was already earmarked to become the State College and today it houses the Charles E. Halbert Library and several divisions (the Division of Arts, Science and General Studies) of the Clarence Fitzroy Bryant College (CFBC) the premier tertiary institution within the Federation of St. Kitts and Nevis.

The induction course was run by the Education Officers of the Department of Education and a number of Canadian Volunteers, who had just arrived to set up the St. Kitts Nevis Teachers College. A number of us who had just left school from the O'level and A'level graduating classes of the Basseterre High School formed the main bulk of the candidates. Amongst us was Henry "Stogumber" Browne.

The course ran for two full weeks with both morning and afternoon sessions. The sessions were very lively and interesting. I fondly remember the instructions of Mr. James Ferguson an education officer from Nevis and Mrs. Ada-Mae Edwards. My mantra which guided my entire career in education was garnered from Mrs. Edwards, "Be firm, fair and friendly" which she had encapsulated as the three F's.

After the selection of the successful candidates for teaching, I was sent to the Sandy Point High School to teach Mathematics and General Science. I arrived at the school on the opening morning of the new school year on the first Monday in September 1968. We received notice of the placement only on the Saturday before the start of school. This gave one practically no time for preparations. Fortunately for me, my father had a number of brand new long sleeved white shirts and two ties in his wardrobe which he graciously gave to me. These were gifts from one of his girl friends who lived in the United Kingdom. I had bought two dress pants in Trinidad; I used the darker one. My shoe was of black leather and relatively new. I had purchased them to travel with to Trinidad, just in case we might have had any formal functions to attend. I was dressed almost brand new for my debut occasion as a teacher. I journeyed to Sandy Point by way of public transport, the minivans, not knowing exactly where the school was. I was guided by the bus driver and shortly thereafter I arrived at the headmaster's office to find my friend and classmate Henry "Stogumber" Browne already awaiting the principal, Mr. R. J. Manchester. We greeted each other, and had some time together and reminisced on the recent past. We were eventually invited into the Principal's office and shortly thereafter we were joined by another first-timer, Eric E. Williams, who was to teach Technical Drawing. We were welcomed by Mr. Manchester and he gave us a fatherly lecture of what was expected of us as he emphasised on the dos and don'ts. We were taken to the staffroom and introduced to a number of teachers. Our friend Eustace "Swing" Arrindell was there in the welcoming party. The Trinity of 'Bouncin, Swing and Stogumber' had its genesis at Sandy Point High.

Eustace had a Morris Oxford motor car P 190 which became the official transport of the Trinity. At mornings Swing would pick up Stogumber, who lived three or four houses to the west of him in Dorset and then travel westward on Cayon Street to pick me up at the junction of Cayon Street and Shaw Avenue. We never had an idle moment on our journeys to and from Sandy Point High. The conversations covered the entire spectrum of world affairs, local events and the runnings with the fairer sex. One of our favourite exploits on our journeys to and from Sandy Point was speed racing; Swing thought he was the Stirling Moss of the St. Kitts roads, and pushed the old Morris Oxford to its limits on many occasions. We were furious when we could not catch-up with or over take another vehicle.

Stogumber and I shared the same desk in the staff room. We had lunch together in the Home Economics Centre daily along with many other teachers who lived outside of Sandy Point. At lunchtime Henry and I were always joined by another new teacher at the school, a graduate teacher Julie Woodley, who had recently graduated from Waterloo University in Canada and had come to the school to head the Geography Department. We shared amongst us three whatever we had for lunch. Julie always had something special to share. That continued for the academic year 1968-69. The lunch bunch was disintegrated thereafter; Henry went to UWI Cave Hill to read for a BA in Liberal Arts, Julie was transferred to Charlestown, Nevis to teach at the Charlestown Secondary and yours truly was transferred to the Basseterre High School.

The year at Sandy Point High had some exciting highlights. The Christmas vacation came at the end of the first term. The school had organized the end of term fair and dance, which was all part of the pre-Christmas activities and they served as major fund raisers for the school. Members of staff were assigned different tasks for the fair and dance. I was responsible for horoscope; a farce which was really only designed for entertainment. We took the statements about love, luck and fortune, from the horoscope sections of various newspapers and magazines. We typed them out on bits of paper, folded them and then placed them in different bags made from black satin. The participants paid five cents for a dip in the bag which matched their Zodiac sign. People had fun just reading the nonsense. We had a public address system over which we mimicked a radio station; playing top hits and sending out requests. Persons at the fair paid five cents for a request form, and would fill in the name of the person to whom they wanted to send the request, the name of the song and the name of the person from whom it was coming. The requests came most of the times from a secret admirer. Songs on the request chart were tunes like: Elvis Presley's—I can't help falling in love with you, the Beatles—I want to hold your hands and Paul Anka's—Please help me I'm falling in love with you. Stogumber was the big announcer on the SPHS Radio. I helped Stogumber with the announcements. Amongst the persons making requests I saw a young lady who had placed as a runner-up in the Miss Rural-West Beauty Queen Show (Half-Way—Tree to Sandy Point to Dieppe Bay). This show was a part of the pre-Christmas Festivities, the winner of the rural districts participated in the final show with three other contestants from Basseterre for the Miss St. Kitts title. The final show was to be held at Warner Park Festival Grounds, the fore—runner to Carnival Village. I invited this young lady into the studio for an interview. I must have had said something that was magical to this young lady. By the evening at the dance, she never allowed me to miss a dance tune. She shadowed me for the entire evening and night. We became very good friends and we limed for most of the Christmas season until her boyfriend banished her from my company.

The Trinity or the Three Musketeers as some termed us, decided to travel to Montserrat for the first week of the Christmas vacation. We went by plane, direct flight by a LIAT 14 seat Twin Otter aircraft at a cost of twenty seven dollars Eastern Caribbean Currency for the round trip. We were accommodated by two friends of 'Swing' whom he had met at a Leeward Island Defence Forces and Cadet Corps combined camp some years earlier. Both David and George were bachelors and lived alone. George had his two bedroom concrete house in Amersham and David lived in rented quarters in Plymouth. Swing and Stogumber slept at George's house and I was given David's one bedroom apartment for sleeping. David was never at home on evenings or nights. He was always out either at work or at his girlfriend's. The place for the day's activities was at George's house. We cooked and ate there. We had a lot of fond memories of that trip. Swing and I had targeted girlfriends from Montserrat.

A former Miss Montserrat who grew up in St. Kitts at the time when her father was stationed there as a member of the Leeward Island Police Force, was Swing's 'chossle'-one of the code terms we used in the Trinity. We got to Montserrat and all was fine. Then there was to be a big Christmas Festivities event at the Vue Pointe Hotel, a formal affair. We got coats to borrow. We were all dressed and waiting on transportation to go. We noticed a motor car drive past George's house and stopped two houses away. The top DJ and radio announcer on Montserrat had arrived at the home of Swing's 'chossle' to take her to the event. When Swing saw her coming down the steps, and realized that the DJ had come to take out his date, he became furious. He ran to the house and barred the young lady from entering the car, and demanded an explanation for the apparent boycott of our plans. She apologised, promised an explanation later, hoping that Swing would let up. Stogumber and I looked from the distance that separated about three house lots away. After about twenty minutes of haggling, the young lady decided that she would go back to her home. Shortly thereafter, a shower of rain precipitated on Montserrat. The rain put a damper on the entire evening. We sat on George's verandah commenting on the events that had just unfolded. It was fun for Stogumber and me but fury for Swing. He told us he gave her an ultimatum in classical style; which was ". . . Choose ye this day whom you will serve". She chose neither but walked back to her parent's home. It was the first time that I saw Swing being defeated; I guess that he would not see that as a defeat but rather as a draw.

My friend was a long standing pen-pal. She was a country girl who lived all the way in Farms Village, the last stop before the airport on the edge of the Atlantic Ocean, across the island from the capital Plymouth. It was difficult to see her. We arranged for us to meet at the Memorial Square in the centre of Plymouth. We would walk back to David's place, our hang out, on two or three occasions. Transportation within the city was not difficult, as the Montserratian folks were very friendly especially to strangers and would always stop and offer a ride if one seemed to be travelling in their direction.

When we were preparing to go to the big cultural event, all three of us decided to use a small quantity of hair straightener to give us what we called a blow-out. My friends over loaded my hair with the chemical and for a while it looked Indo-Pakistani, but the true nature of my African knotties did not maintain it for long. The outing in Montserrat was exciting. On some occasions we had the full use of a car which belonged to some one of our friends. We covered the entire landscape of Montserrat. Swing was always the official driver. We returned to St. Kitts on Christmas Eve. I was anxious to meet my new friend from the school show and dance. She was not difficult to find even in the mass of persons that invaded the city on Christmas Eve night. Maybe we had the same objectives.

Swing and Stogumber were the sharp ones when it came to dealing with the fairer sexes. I was awfully slow compared to them. They hunted for and spotted every opening. I guess I had one staring in my face that I did not see, right there in the staff room. I was heckled and ridiculed by my two best friends for my naivety until I was straightened out by the young woman herself. We became close friends for the best part of the next two years. I travelled to Nevis often. In all our dealings Swing and Stogumber were the aggressors and I was the voice of conscience. I have promised both of them, that in the eternity, I will beg for a day off from hell for both of them.

We had a flourishing drama group in place. All three of us participated. We were requested to produce a fifteen minutes humorous skit as part of the side show for the Miss Western Rural Queen show which was held at the auditorium of the Sandy Point High School. I wrote the script and directed the skit, casting the Trinity, along with another young staff member Aubrey Hart and a young lady Marilyn Dickenson who had made several stage appearances with us. That sketch was re-witten in 1976 and now stands as a One Act Comedy in the name "It's only for a Time". Stogumber and I also worked with a theatre group under the Direction of Eustace Esdaille. In April of 1969 we staged a production called "Life with a Halo"—a biographical depiction of the life of Martin Luther King Jr. This was all part of the black consciousness which had engulfed our interest. It was the time when Hewey Newton, Eldridge Cleaver, Stokely Carmichael, Malcolm X and MLK were our heroes. We were Black Power Advocates, Black and Proud. Stogumber played the lead role as MLK and I played the part as one of his aides. It was a fantastic production that involved both singing and straight drama; we packed the Basseterre High School Auditorium for several showings for both adults and children. After the successful runs in St. Kitts we went to Nevis and performed it to a packed audience in the auditorium of the Charlestown Secondary School. We got tremendous reviews in the local newspapers.

We planned a hike to Mount Misery, renamed Mount Liamuiga, for staff and some senior students of the Sandy Point High School for a Sunday morning around the Easter weekend of 1969. The plan was to meet at the school then drive down to Belmont Estate, get a ride by way of tractor to the foot hill of Mount Misery and hike uphill to the crater and back down. Swing, a mutual friend named Leonard "Macaroni" Leader and I set out that morning from Basseterre in Swing's motor car P 190. When we got to SPHS the hiking party had already left. We were about an hour late. When we got to Belmont Estate the group had already left by way of tractor to the foot hills. Swing decided that he would drive as far up the beaten track of mud, wash outs and humps as far as we could make it. He pushed and coaxed the old Morris Oxford to its limits. At one point the rear end of the car got stuck on the ridge of a hump. We had to stop and push the car backwards in order to prevent it from blocking the road. We secured the car and started walking towards the foot hills. On our way up the tractor from Belmont Estate passed us on its way down. The driver shouted to us that group was about a half hour ahead of us.

We got into the forest and followed the visible track. We climbed for about an hour and a half before we heard any sound or saw any motion of the group. We decided that we would not call the group but would walk quietly behind them and that when we had almost reached the summit, we would make our own path to the rim of the crater. That proved to be a bad decision. We left the fresh trails of the group ahead, which had an experienced guide with them. We went to the right of the track and started to make our own tracks with the hope of reaching the crater rim before them. At one time we found ourselves stuck on a ridge, with a precipice of over two hundred feet that ended in a deep gorge. There and then we decided that we were lost and would start our descent back into safety.

We backed away from the cliff and walked down hill through the thick rainforest. We kept our spirits up by pretending as if we were reporters from the local media giving details of a search and rescue activity which was focused on us. We had food, and drank water from a number of natural springs. For over three hours we struggled downhill with great uncertainty. We followed the basin of a ravine with one certainty that it would eventually take us to the sea. We swung on vines to get over some difficult areas and slid on our backsides to get down some steep inclines. At one point when we were walking on the actual water course, I had disturbed some rocks and my left leg went through a cavity in the bed of the water course way up to above my knee. I paused for a moment as my two companions looked at me in shock and disbelief. My first thought was how long I would have to stay there until help would reach me, if my leg was broken. I was with "Swing" and "Macaroni" whose combined weights were less than my own. I tried wiggling my toes, no problem with that, and then I started to pump my leg up and down, I then realized that I was all right except for some bruises on the leg and knee. My friends helped me free myself by moving away some of the stones; I was freed and we continued our journey downwards. Occasionally we would come out of the ravine to explore for tracks. On one such occasion we found some tracks and followed them that took us back to the point where we had entered the rainforest. We walked back to Swings car and made our way back to Belmont Estate.

That was my second journey to the crater of Mount Misery. The first was a field trip with Mr. David Wright's geography class when I was in fourth form. That trip was successful as we were compelled to follow all instructions and stayed with the group. We reached the summit, had something to eat and water to refresh ourselves, and later descended into the crater. The walls of the crater descended at an angle in excess of eighty degrees. We crawled to the bottom. It was an awesome sight at the bottom with a huge crater lake, with areas of flat land that looked like an open pasture. We explored the bottom until we came to the sulphurtara, a huge area where we could see the effusion of steam and smell the sulphurous gases rising from the holes in the ground. There were bubbling mud pools along with deposits of yellow crystalline sulphur on the ground. The vegetation was like none that I had seen before. The plants in the area of the sulphurtara are unique only to that environment of high concentrations of sulphurous gases. Some persons brought eggs and poached them in the hot mud pools. Legend had it that if any number of eggs were placed in the mud pools the mountain would take at least one for itself. The legend never played out for us because all the eggs that were put in were recovered. The trek back up to the rim out of the crater was the most difficult part as we had to use both toes and fingers to claw ourselves out of the steep inclined walls. The roots of the trees on the walls of the crater provided support for our exit from the crater. The climb back down the mountain then was routine and uneventful. I made my third trip to Mount Misery some years after I returned home from university.

During the last term of the academic year 68-69 the fifth form repeaters of the Basseterre High School, decided that they wanted an adventure like we had by going down the Eastern Caribbean and Trinidad on one of the Federal ships. They invited Stogumber and me to be part of their advisory committee for fund raising and planning. We worked with them. They did not raise enough money for the Eastern Caribbean and Trinidad trip so they adjusted their plans and went to Jamaica for a ten day trip. Jamaica was just one stop from St. Kitts. The fares were computed on the number of stops one would make on their journey; I can recall it was a basic cost of thirty dollars and ten dollars for every stop. It cost Stogumber and me forty dollars each for the boat ride and we paid some additional monies for accommodation at Taylor Hall, Mona Campus of UWI, Jamaica.

We left St. Kitts on a Saturday night early in August 1969 on the Federal Maple for our second Caribbean Tour. My twenty-first birthday was spent on the Federal Maple sailing between Puerto Rico and Hispaniola. We sailed for three full days before docking at Kingston. On arrival, we took several taxis, four per cab, up to Mona Campus. Our arrangements at Taylor Hall were the same as those we enjoyed at Milner Hall in Trinidad the year before. Jamaica was fun. The fruits of Papene Market and the language of the Jamaicans were so exciting. We visited the zoo and the botanical gardens that were not very far from the campus. We took the Jamaica Transport Board buses to Kingston and Half-Way-Tree every day. We did not venture outside of Kingston and its environs. The first time I swam in a swimming pool was at Mona Campus. We had a good and friendly bunch of persons on that tour, much more cohesive or copasetic, as we would say, than the group that we had travelled with to Trinidad the year before. We built lasting friendships with many members of the group; to this day Ian 'Patches' Liburd always greets Stogumber and me as "Jack"; a name we coined on that trip. I could remember going to the straw market in downtown Kingston and buying two top quality straw baskets with brown leather trimmings and flaps with brass latches. They were identical in design except that one was bigger than the other and chosen in a way to match the physical sizes of the ladies for whom they were intended. I paid thirty two shilling and twenty eight shillings for the respective sizes; Jamaica was still using the old sterling currency of pounds, shillings and pence. One was taken to Nevis and the other was given to a pastors' daughter, inside of which was placed a note in Latin, which read "Te amo". The relationship with the pastor's daughter never went beyond a walk home from school, many hours of sitting on the verandah talking about world affairs and doing mathematics home work.

At the start of the academic year 69-70 I was transferred from Sandy Point High to Basseterre High. Swing left for the College of the Virgin Islands. With my two main conspirators gone, I was pretty much on my own. Russell Best became a closer friend of mine during that year. He limed with Stogumber and me on several occasions. We travelled to all parts of the country for dances and other activities. He had access to his family car P2038 on evenings. I could remember one night we went to a steel band dance at the St. Peters Anglican Schoolroom, when a young woman held on to Russell and danced with him for most of the night. He had introduced himself to the young lady as Jonathon Swift. "Swift" became his name within the grouping after that.

At Basseterre High there was a marked shortage of science teachers as many of the expected English VSO's had not arrived. I was given a challenge by the then headmaster, one of my mentors, Eustace Esdaille, to teach additional mathematics to the lower sixth form as well as chemistry and mathematics in fourth and third forms. Mr. Sydney Osborne was over loaded with the upper sixth form pure and applied mathematics, as well as the upper and lower sixth forms for physics and the fifth form physics. I took on the challenge with some doubts and reservations. I could not let the confidence placed in me by my mentor be in vain. It was a big class. Names like Sheila Bass, Mignon Guishard, Gwen King, Willa Franks, Eugene Welsh, Douglas Woodley and Patrick Ribeiro were members of a twenty strong class. We prevailed and returned better grades, both in quantity and quality, than the class of the year before, which had been taught by a graduate VSO. Many of these students did extremely well later on in university; of special note was Sheila Bass who got first class honours at UWI, Cave Hill in Mathematics and Economics.

While at Basseterre High I walked across the city from Mc Knight along my old accustomed route as a school boy. I started to take extreme pride in my outfits for school. I wore the styles that were fashionable and mixed and matched appropriately. I could remember an outfit that I wore from time to time; forest green shoes, moss green trousers and olive green shirt with a lime green tie. They were all of different hues of green, those were the days when we "sheeked", a term we used for stylish dressing. In those days I began to find it difficult to walk all the way back to Mc Knight for lunch. Instead I bought lunch in town. My favourite stop was at Euclid's on Central Street.

I can remember many afternoons timing when a young lady, who taught at the Girls' School and who went for lunch in Irish Town, would be returning so as to get a walk and talk on our way back to school. The interest grew between us. From time to time she would actually walk across Central Street to make our rendezvous surer. I was always complimented for my dress, and so I dressed even more immaculately to impress. The current of friendship ran deep and remained platonic for that year. We also had reason to interact on occasions when Young Labour, the youth arm of the St. Kitts Nevis Labour Party, started to introduce classes for certification in the Local School Leaving Examinations for persons who had left school without any form of certification.

The National School Leaving Certificate would help one to get jobs as a police constable, join the army and work as a clerks in some areas of the private businesses and the government sector and as messengers. It also provided a means that verified that one had had some form of formal education. I was sent to teach Mathematics in the evenings twice weekly at the Trinity/Boyd's branch of Young Labour at the Trinity School. The President of the Young Labour Branch there was Cynthia 'Hya' Cotton. We met on other Young Labour activities, at seminars, conventions and camps. The leadership of the St. Kitts—Nevis Labour Party identified potential leaders of the Labour Movement who were exposed to a lot of political education and we were well grounded in the founding principles of the Labour Movement. It was at a camp of Young Labour at the Verchild's School that we spent hours late into the evening talking about everything. I was not attending the camp as a fulltime camper but rode my bicycle to Verchild's and camped there overnight. By then I had secured entrance to the Cave Hill Campus, UWI, Barbados. Some time just before lights out in the camp I asked this young lady if she could wait for three to four years while I was away in Barbados. The answer was in the affirmative and confirmed our relationship.

CHAPTER 12

The Christena Disaster

The holiday weekend, centred on the first Monday in August 1970, was to be a time when many persons journeyed to Nevis for the festive occasions of August Monday. There were to be many fetes over the weekend and horse racing on August Monday. Russell and Stogumber and I, planned to be in Nevis for that weekend.

The plan was that at sometime over the weekend we would travel to Nevis. My plan was to travel on the Saturday, August 01 on the afternoon trip via the MV Christena. In those days, it was customary for me to take a food package of the basic staples, salt fish and other provisions on Saturdays to Newtown for my Grandmother Narna. I went there relatively early that Saturday. When I got there after the usual greetings, she reminded me that I had promised to fix a fence for her. I promised that I would fix the fence the next Saturday as I had plans to travel to Nevis on the same day. My grandmother was vocal in her attack on me, calling me ungrateful amongst other things. I was embarrassed about the situation so I decided to do some kind of patchwork on the fence. I started to do some work on the fence which was to be a temporary arrangement. My short cut methods eventually resulted in the total collapse of the section of the fence which I intended to repair. I opted then to save the arguing and harassment from my grandmother. I decided that I would do the right thing and fix the fence properly. I had to replant supporting poles, attach runners and remount the galvanized sheetings. The task took me an extra three hours, all the while angry with my grandmother for detaining me that long. The loss of time meant that I would not be able to go back to Mc Knight to organise myself so that I could catch the ferry and go over to Nevis. I had settled in my mind that I would wait for the special excursion trip which was organized for August Monday.

I was at my home in Mc Knight listening to a regional netball game that was being played in Dominica. Sometime, there was an interruption by the announcer on the radio who said that the MV Christena had gone down in the channel between St. Kitts and Nevis. That was an announcement that struck me like a rod of lightening. I could not believe what I was hearing. That was the end of the netball game for me. I got to the Bay Front and observed a number of fishermen pushing their crafts into the water as to be part of the rescue mission. Here I was wondering if Russell was on the boat, but shortly afterwards I found out that he was safe, for by then I had seen him on the bay front. My concern about other friends and relatives who might have been on the trip grew.

A number of persons had come to the Bay Front. We stood there staring out to sea for hours. After darkness a number of helicopters from the US military base in Puerto Rico came in to join the rescue mission. They dropped flares that emitted brilliant light to help with the vision of the night-time search and rescue operations. We looked at the flares as they fell from distances high above the surface back into the sea. That in itself was a spectacle to behold. The rumours of who had been rescued alive made the rounds amongst us as we looked on. ZIZ Radio was very instrumental in keeping the country informed about the various developments and persons used it as a means of communicating with each other as to who was alright or otherwise.

A number of medical doctors and other personnel wanted to go to Nevis with medical supplies and other bits of equipment to help out with the situation. There was an aeroplane on the airport at Golden Rock that was detained there by the government; the reason for the detention of the aircraft I never knew. Some negotiations between the owners of the aircraft and the government took place within a short period of time. It was agreed that the aircraft would be allowed to be used for taking the emergency supplies and personnel to Nevis. The air strip at New Castle, Nevis was not lighted for night-time landing, so a makeshift arrangement for lighting the area of the strip had to be formulated. It was decided that a number of motor cars should line the boundaries of the airstrip with the headlamps on, pointing in the opposite direction from where the aircraft would normally land. This information was communicated on ZIZ radio and within an hour there were sufficient volunteers with their motor cars at New Castle Airport to provide the lighting needed for the landing of the aircraft. The plane was piloted by a local pilot by the name of Derrick Thompson. The takeoff and landing were successful and both personnel and supplies got over safely.

I guess I retired from the Bay Front sometime in the small hours of Sunday morning. By mid-morning I was back at the Bay Front. By then a number of bodies had been recovered and they were stored in a makeshift morgue at the Alexandra Hospital on Nevis. A number of blocks of ice, stored in sawdust, were brought to the Treasury Pier and loaded on to a motor launch to go over to Nevis. I helped with the loading and journeyed to Nevis on the motor launch with the ice. The launch was captained by my brother-in-law, Joshua Halliday, so I had no difficulty getting on. The boat ride was for about an hour and fifteen minutes. We off loaded the ice onto a flat bed truck which was already at the pier by the time we arrived in Nevis. We arrived at the hospital and were directed to the makeshift morgue in a bottom floor room. I saw the corpses of over thirty persons, including three Catholic nuns and a number of persons whom I knew, stretched out on the bare concrete floor. We proceeded by removing the ice blocks from the bags with saw dust and strategically placed them so that they could keep the temperature down to a minimum, so as to reduce the rate of decomposition of the corpses.

I was back and forth for that day throughout Nevis. I eventually reached the home of my friend. That place where I had been scheduled to stay for that weekend but under much different circumstances. There were endless calls coming in and going out from the telephone at the house. We made a log of the names of persons about whom enquiries were made. We would relay information from various individuals and agencies of the government including the Police and ZIZ Radio.

Stogumber had travelled to Nevis the day before. Russell had not bothered to go to Nevis as he had not made final contact with either Stogumber or me. I spent the night in Nevis. The next day Stogumber and I returned to St. Kitts, not by sea but by air. By then we were hearing the stories of the sightings of large quantities of sharks in the water around the channel area where the Christena had sunk. When we got to the airport at New Castle, Nevis we met the then Chief Minister of Montserrat, Hon. W. Bramble, who had arrived in Nevis to have a firsthand view of the disaster that had struck his neighbouring comrades. For the next three days I volunteered my services ferrying dead bodies from the Treasury Pier in Basseterre to the Springfield Cemetery. Coffins were made by cutting plywood sheets into the appropriate lengths and width and nailing them into rectangular boxes. Trenches were dug by bulldozers at the Springfield Cemetery that served as mass graves for the bodies that were recovered from the sea. A British Frigate and a French Minesweeper aided unreservedly in the rescue mission. The last body that was recovered was that of Captain Ponteen, the Master of the ill fated vessel. By the end of the rescue operations my right hand became swollen. What caused it I? I never found out. I went to the out-patient division of the J N France hospital and received an injection that seemed to set things right again.

It has been said that ninety-nine persons survived the tragedy and some two hundred and fifty six souls perished. My number was definitely not in that bundle that was to be called to the great beyond. I gave thanks and prayers to my grandmother for her insistence and to fate for prolonging the repairs to the fence that eventually deterred me from joining the MV Christena on her final voyage. If I had gone on the ferry that day the statistics would have been different. It would have been one hundred survived and two hundred and fifty six perished.

CHAPTER 13

National Arts Festival 1970

The National Arts Festival of 1970 had a significant impact on my career in Theatre Arts. The performing arts were centred at the Basseterre High School grounds where a huge open air stage was erected. The festival was the brain child of the Hon. C A P Southwell who was then Deputy Premier and Minister of Finance etc. and the chairman of the festival committee was William F Dore. One of the major attractions of the festival was a production of Shakespeare's "Julius Caesar". It was produced within a contemporary setting. A theatre specialist, Slade Hopkinson was invited from Trinidad to direct the play. The cast was packed with many persons of national note. The Hon. C A P Southwell played the part of Mark Anthony; Leroy Nelson played Julius Caesar, Henry "Stogumber" Browne played the part of Cassius, Hon. Lee L Moore played the part of the Captain that drove the crowd from the streets that were in festive mood and the celebrations had the Coco Cola Coronets Steel Band jamming across the stage. I had a minor part, being a stage hand and a member of the crowd. I attended most of the rehearsal sessions and garnered many of the techniques used by the experienced director. I was amazed by the style and thoroughness of Slade Hopkinson.

One of the featured events of the Arts Festival was a presentation on local folklore coupled with local superstitions. I was given instructions to write and produce a skit based on stories about an obeahman from Nevis. I called the skit "King Marssa". I played the lead role as the obeahman and relied heavily on my knowledge of chemistry to deceive the audience into believing that King Marssa had real mystic powers. The cast included Junie Liburd as the Governor, Angela Clark as a rich business woman, and Marilyn Dickenson as a battered wife and Eustace "Swing" Arrindell as the other obeahman. This play had a profound impact on the audience to the extent that one woman actually telephoned me after the production to enquire if she could engage me to help her control her husband. My performance in "King Marssa" brought me into national prominence. Many doors were opened to me.

Sometime in September of 1970 I went to the office of the Permanent Secretary of the Ministry of Establishment and Human Resources to deliver a letter in which I was requesting study leave so that I could go to university. The Permanent Secretary then was a lady who was well versed in the Fine Arts. I was granted permission to see her in her office and as I entered she offered me a seat and proceeded to talk about the Arts Festival. Our conversation went on for over half an hour before she asked me what was it that I had really come to her office to talk about. I stated my mission. She asked me a few personal questions and then proceeded to draft a letter which she completed and then handed it to me and asked me to take the letter to her personal secretary to type and further instructed me to return in the afternoon to affix my signature. All this time I already had my letter of application for study leave drafted and signed in my pocket; I made no mention of it. I was granted study leave without pay for the duration of my studies at UWI, Cave Hill Campus, Barbados.

CHAPTER 14

Off To University

I was not time-tabled on the Basseterre High School Staff allocations for the new school year as I had only three weeks before going off to university. All the members of staff who were university bound were deployed to a number of primary schools to substitute for teachers until the final allocations of new teachers were done. I was sent to the Verchild's All Age School to teach for the three weeks prior to going to Barbados. As fate would have it, when I arrived at Verchild's I was shocked and amazed to see Miss Cynthia Cotton there awaiting the Principal, Miss Warner. I enquired of "Hya" what she was doing there. I was informed that she had been transferred from the Girl's School in Basseterre. That gave us three more weeks of consolidation of our friendship. I had done an evaluation of this young woman and she scored high on every category evaluated. I judged her character from the pleasant and humble personality of her mother. I thought that she had the traits that would make her the ideal wife and mother.

When I told my father that I was making plans to go to University, we started a discussion about fees and support. I gave my father my Bank of America pass book which had a positive balance of twenty two hundred dollars plus interest. I had saved one hundred dollars every month of my two years working as a Non-Graduate Assistant Teacher except for the two Decembers. My father said that he was surprised. He thought that I was just out for fun and games and never realized that I was saving so much money and had interest in further studies. He promised that he would give me whatever support he could.

I was first accepted by the College of the Virgin Islands. I had also applied to the University of the West Indies and had also written the UWI scholarship examinations. When I got admission to CVI, Swing was elated. Early in September, I was notified that I got accepted to UWI-Cave Hill campus to do a B.Sc. in Natural Sciences and was awarded a British Development Scholarship for four years of study. Naturally I opted for the one with the scholarship and joined Stogumber in Barbados.

On the eve of my leaving for Barbados I went to West Farm to say goodbye. I was driven by my friend Russell. The goodbye was brief as Hya was in pain with a swollen leg, suffering from a centipede sting that she had received the evening before.

I left St. Kitts, university bound on Sunday, October 2, 1970. It was another first in all our family's generations.

Me at 13 SKNGS uniform

Bouncin' at 19

Bouncin' and Angela Clark

Bouncin' and Eustace 'Swing' Arrindell

Bouncin' and Juni Liburd

Bouncin' and Marilyn Dickenson

Mom and Dad wedding day

Cynthia 'Hya' Cotton (1970)

Henry and Bouncin'

Basseterre Boys' School

St. Kitts Nevis Grammar School

St. Kitts Sugar Factor(Basseterre)Ltd

Wesley Methodist Church- Seaton Street, Basseterre